Books by Catherine Drinker Bowen

HISTORY OF LEHIGH UNIVERSITY

THE STORY OF THE OAK TREE

RUFUS STARBUCK'S WIFE *a novel*

FRIENDS AND FIDDLERS

BELOVED FRIEND
The Story of Tchaikowsky and Nadejda von Meck
(*In Collaboration with B. von Meck*)

FREE ARTIST
The Story of Anton and Nicholas Rubinstein

YANKEE FROM OLYMPUS
Justice Holmes and His Family

JOHN ADAMS AND THE AMERICAN REVOLUTION

THE WRITING OF BIOGRAPHY *an essay*

THE LION AND THE THRONE
The Life and Times of Sir Edward Coke

ADVENTURES OF A BIOGRAPHER

FRANCIS BACON
The Temper of a Man

MIRACLE AT PHILADELPHIA
The Story of the Constitutional Convention,
May to September 1787

BIOGRAPHY: THE CRAFT AND THE CALLING

IOGRAPHY:
The Craft and the Calling

by CATHERINE DRINKER BOWEN

 IOGRAPHY:
The Craft and the
Calling

GREENWOOD PRESS, PUBLISHERS
WESTPORT, CONNECTICUT

Library of Congress Cataloging in Publication Data

Bowen, Catherine Drinker, 1897-
    Biography : the craft and the calling.

    Reprint of the ed. published by Little, Brown,
Boston.
    Includes index.
    1. Biography (as a literary form). I. Title.
[CT21.B564 1978]   808'.066'92   77-19110
ISBN 0-313-20219-2

Reprinted by permission of Little, Brown and Company in
association with the Atlantic Monthly Press

Reprinted in 1978 by Greenwood Press, Inc.,
51 Riverside Avenue, Westport, Conn. 06880

Printed in the United States of America

For Barbara Rex

Foreword

People like to say that writing cannot be taught. If they
mean that talent cannot be taught they are correct of
course. Talent can only be discovered, prodded, encour-
aged or shamed to action. But where technique is concerned, surely it is teachable in any art. "If you own a
hundred thousand francs' worth of craftsmanship,"
Degas told a pupil, "spend five sous to buy more."
Writers can learn much from good editors, though good

editors are few and far between. To this day I remember and follow certain dicta pronounced at the Bread Loaf Writers Conference by Bernard De Voto more than thirty years ago. A group of us sat on the steps of the Inn. I was embarrassed because De Voto, a staff member whom I had that morning met for the first time, was reading a short story of mine. De Voto's pencil was in his hand and he let his friends know exactly what was wrong with my pages. "You say everything twice," he told me, and dug the pencil through two lines. "Sounds Biblical. 'By the waters of Babylon I laid me down. I laid me down by the waters of Babylon.' With you it's always better the second time. Overwriting is tolerable in a first draft," he went on, and handed me the manuscript. "Just run this through your typewriter again," he said.

First draft? I had written that story countless times. But I would not take a hundred dollars for what De Voto taught me. Years later, shortly before he died, De Voto read another manuscript of mine, a book, this time. "You are writing more simply," he said. "As we grow older this should happen. There is no time left for anything but the ultimate simplicities."

In the course of a writing life I have lectured on history and biography from many platforms. Afterward I have often felt that it was in the question period that we came closest to the issues. How do you decide whom to write about? — they ask. Is the research all done before you start writing or as you go along? Do you choose your heroes because you like them, and have you ever written about a man you despised? What happens when you come upon a period in the subject's life where material is scarce or nonexistent? Do you ever find yourself blocked and how do you recover?

After years of such questions it seemed expedient to go further and answer them once and for all in a book. And because the questions — and the problems involved — were directed to my personal experience as a writer, I have naturally referred on occasion to my own biographies, though not with the assumption that the reader knows them; the examples given are self-explanatory. There is a genteel tradition that authors should not talk about their works. Yet while one can admire the books of other writers, envying their talent and their techniques, one cannot tell if, in early drafts, these authors found themselves stopped, or how they contrived to climb out of their particular literary mire. As illustrations of excellence and how things are at their highest level, I use in great part four books: *Mary Tudor,* by Hilda F. M. Prescott; *Elizabeth the Great,* by Elizabeth Jenkins; *The Young Melbourne,* by David Cecil; *The Armada,* by Garrett Mattingly. That two were written by women, two by men, is incidental; incidental also that three of the authors are English, though indeed it has seemed to me that English biographers are notably concerned with style, the turn of a sentence and such matters as the sustaining of a book's tone throughout. *The Armada,* properly speaking, is history. Yet its every page holds lessons for the biographer. Beyond the volumes named, my examples actually range far; some are recent, some older. If I have stressed the four it is simply because I learned from them; they are an intrinsic part of my writing experience. I would hope that readers will supply their own examples as we go along, books they admire and that spring to mind.

To search over men's work — surely it comes under the head of learning, of being taught to write? The biographer goes to the masters not only for style or "inspiration." He looks for help on specific points: how do these books open, how do they close? How many chapters have they; is the subject's youth described, is the reader present at his death? Is there conversation, and how does the author handle his citations for quoted material — in footnotes or chapter notes or not at all? Never mind if one has met these questions before, and answered them. Each book one writes is different in content and therefore in form; with each book old problems present themselves in guises new and strange.

And beyond this searching of the masters' finished products, one seeks out their personal statements as writers, their confessions and counsels. Let us say the biographer's research period is finished. In his typewriter sits a blank sheet of paper. "Chapter One," it says at the top. Awesome words, fit to bring any serious writer to a stumbling halt. Already the masters' works have been referred to; at this crucial point one needs something more intimate: did they too suffer blocks and frustrations? I have a collection of books on writing; down they come from their shelves, among them *The Journals* of Gamaliel Bradford; Nancy Hale on *The Realities of Fiction;* E. M. Forster's *Aspects of the Novel;* C. V. Wedgwood's *Truth and Opinion;* R. J. Collingwood's *The Idea of History;* Mary Roberts Rinehart's brief intense confession called *Writing Is*

Work. It does not matter that Forster wrote magnificent fiction and Rinehart wrote detective stories, whereas I plan the biography of a sixteenth-century lawyer which will contain no word of fiction. The problems of construction are basically the same. "I have produced over fifty books," says Mrs. Rinehart, "uncounted articles and editorials and have produced seven plays. Every one of them has disappointed me; many bitterly, some less than others . . . the more easily anything reads, the harder it has been to write. There is no such thing as light-hearted spontaneous creation, save in the mind, before it is set down on paper."

Mrs. Rinehart was an honest craftsman, skillful and successful in what she undertook, and ready to persist against great odds. She wrote on a kitchen table with her children milling round; she wrote on hospital beds before dangerous operations. "It is frequently necessary," she says, "to work against extremely adverse conditions."

The job is to get something down on paper. Chapter One, Chapter Two; for better or worse let the typewriter roll. We need pages in the hand to work with, ponder over, rewrite, reshape. One thinks of Mr. Prufrock; " 'Do I dare?' and, 'Do I dare?' "

Some years ago I published a little book called *Adventures of a Biographer,* about biographical research, the out-and-indoor sport of traveling through the world to read in foreign libraries, interview persons involved and walk where my subjects, my heroes, had walked. The present book is wholly concerned with how a writer puts a book together, the problem of setting it on paper economically, vividly, with clarity and narrative continuity. An occasional sentence or literary example has been borrowed from magazine articles of mine or a brief published lecture called *The Writing of Biography*. But what a writer believed in 1950 or 1958 she may well have outgrown by 1969; this book is a new statement. Before my first biography, *Beloved Friend,* appeared, I had published magazine fiction, a novel, a book of essays on music, and had held a job on a daily newspaper. For better or worse therefore, what I have to say about writing was learned in various media and applies equally, I think, to these media.

Writing a full-length biography is a long and difficult task, during which one is possessed not by dreams of glory but by anxiety. Misrepresentation of the subject occurs not only through factual error and the quoting of doubtful sources but by faulty organization, the clumsy construction of page, paragraph or sentence. Once a book is finished, published, the nightmare dissipates and the writer dismisses these technical problems as a mother proverbially forgets the pangs of birth. To revive them is a doubtful pleasure. If I have chosen to do so I can only hope my testimony will be of use.

Contents

Contents

IOGRAPHY:
The Craft and the Calling

1.

 lotting the biography

A novelist informed me, with magisterial assurance, that compared to fiction writers, biographers have an easy time. Their plot is ready to hand before they even begin to write. When I asked, what plot, exactly? — the novelist said it was self-evident: "Birth, education, marriage, career, death."

Surely the novelist was mistaken, and his five neat sequential nouns indicated a chronology rather than a plot? Consider Monday, for instance, which has its beginning and ending; the sun rises and sets. One breakfasts, works, lunches, takes a walk, goes out to dinner perhaps, comes home, goes to bed. Yet if a writer wishes to engage a reader's attention concerning Monday, his hero must that day meet with trouble, face an obstacle, a danger, a grief, and conquer it. Or if the writer prefers tragedy, then Monday's obstacle can be conqueror, and draw a reader's tears.

The book trade calls it conflict, suspense. By whatever name it is a quality vital to biography as to fiction. The difference is that the novelist invents his plot, whereas the biographer finds it in history, in actual fact as indicated by the given material, by events as they unfold, and more particularly by the character of the biographical subject, the hero. Maurois has something to say about this. The biographer, he believes, "has greater difficulty than the novelist in composition. But he has one compensation: to be compelled to take over the form of a work ready-made is almost always a source of power to the artist. It is painful, it makes his task more difficult; but at the same time it is from this struggle between the mind and the matter that resists it that a masterpiece is born."

Graduate students of history, having labored for years on a thesis, often feel ambitious to see their work in print. Approaching some available professional writer they inquire how their production can be fixed up for trade publication. "Popular presentation," they have learned to call it.

The professional writer is wary of such assignments.

A biography must be planned *before* it is written, not afterward. Yet as an example, the graduate student's problem can be worth careful inspection because it is actually the same problem the seasoned biographer confronts in the early stages of his books. The material is gathered, now what is to be done with it? These pages — this thesis — dry, correct, with serried footnotes, can be extremely useful as reference on a library shelf. And it covers the ground, certainly. But it moves on mechanized wooden legs, without head or guts, humor or humanity. Yet humor and humanity cannot be stuffed into a book at later convenience but must grow from the narrative as it progresses, springing hot and hearty from the writer's own bias and involvement as he sits and thinks about his subject.

Ask such a graduate student what his thesis, his book, is about. Not merely the name and life schedule of the hero, but what the book is *about,* what is its plot, what carries it along? For answer you will be given a chronology, a train of events. Let us say the biographical subject is an agent for Indian affairs on the American frontier, *circa* 1775. Captain B —— has fought the French, he knows Indians; he is prospering and minding his business, when along comes the Revolution — and he chooses the Tory side.

Divided loyalty! Here is a theme, here is plot enough to carry to the end. For what is biography but the story of a man or woman in conflict with himself? Moreover the subject is fresh; the Tory in our Revolution has not been explored in depth, as the professors say. Yet — take the manuscript in hand and what is presented on the page? Battles, boundary lines, Indian raids, with actual

5

tallies of the scalped and the dead. Footnotes, chapter notes, bibliography. Everything neat, verified — and bloodless even though the scene itself is soaked in blood.

But the man who wrote the thesis is not dry. When he talks about his hero-captain he is entertaining, he is funny; what he says concerning his characters is quick and sharp. One knows of course that such qualities, transferred to the page, are of no help toward graduate honors. Yet this young man has not come to discuss academic degrees. Ask him then, if his hero suffered, if the captain doubted his position and his choice, felt sadness at the loss of old friends among the Americans.

For answer the young man begins to explain what it meant to be a loyalist in the Revolution, and what his captain's soul will lose or gain thereby. Suddenly his every word is gold. Write it down! the professional says. Write it on the back of an envelope, quick, before it vanishes. . . .

There is, one assumes, proof of the captain's struggle, quotations available in letters, diaries, if not from the captain's hand then from someone in a like position. Did the captain have a family and did they share his views and loyalties? More legwork, as the reporters call it, was desirable, but legwork with a different end in view. Canadian libraries might yield a harvest. It would be worthwhile to visit repositories in Ottawa, Detroit. . . . The thesis is filled moreover with names of Indian tribes, Indian chiefs with whom the hero had close dealings. Is there some indirect way of repeating what they said? We must not have fictional conversation around the council fire. But treaties were made with the

6

French, the English. The language is available, it is written down.

The young man had been excellently trained in evaluating evidence. He could spot a bad source, a dubious statement across a library room. In short, he had completed one phase of a biographer's training. But if he aimed beyond the classroom, if he wished the world to read about his hero, his Tory captain, he would find the next phase of training equally rigorous. He must move into the realm of feeling, of men and women and their emotions. Through historical evidence, fortified and animated by his own experience of living, he must pick these people up bodily from his dry pages, turn them over in his hand, stare at them long and searchingly.

And there is a further task, a pleasant one to my way of thinking. It concerns scene. What about terrain, one asks the writer — the rivers, the hills? This is an outdoor story. We must see the hero's country; a Tory captain does not float in air. In the thesis as it stands there is no field or forest or blockhouse or cellar that one can remember or describe after reading — let alone a face, a voice, the figure of a man. The words on the page should be evocative, call up colors, sounds, sights, smells.

This of course is reckless counsel. Not everybody can write a scene or describe a man's face. Not everyone has eyes to see a field, a tree in life, let alone set it down in writing. There is no sense pretending that technique will take the place of talent. Yet here again, practice counts, in perception as in writing. Moreover, at certain stages heroic measures are called for, strong medicine to clear the writer's vision, turn him about to face another direction. He must free himself from his strict specific training, which for its purpose was excellent. Like the student who has mastered the fundamentals of grammar he is prepared, he is ready. Of what he has learned nothing will be forgotten, neglected or distorted. But the time has come to make the material his own, transform it into words that live, that pulse, communicate.

Once the beginner has his plot in mind — his central animating theme — he will do well to think over the chronology of the hero's life, the big things that happened. These he can note down in scenes, as for a stage play but with the dates, keeping always in mind the direction his work is heading, the climax which by now must surely have declared itself. This exercise might fill three or four pages of $8\frac{1}{2}''$ x $11''$ paper. Then he can begin to write his book, working from scene to scene, as the composer of a symphony heads for the next theme, whether a secondary subject or a development.

So simplified a program will not of course make a book. But it is a step taken, a map, a way out of the wilderness of research into a final choice of incident. It leads from the library into life, narration, drama, plot. An outline need not, however, be a rigid plan that must be followed letter for letter. Indeed, I have seen biographical outlines so complete, so detailed and heavy they bade fair to crush the story, deceiving the author into thinking he had written his book. What one advocates is a loose chronology which reads vividly simply because the incidents, the characters or occasional quotations from hero or heroine are themselves vivid. For example, Queen Elizabeth, as a young woman, "told

8

the French Ambassador de Foix that whenever she thought about marriage, she felt as if someone were tearing the heart out of her bosom." Again, to her ladies, on hearing that Mary Stuart had born a child: "The Queen of Scots is lighter of a fair son, and I am but a barren stock."

When Miss Jenkins came across those words in the records, surely her mind leaped forward, imagining the time and place where she could set them in her book.

It is easier to tell someone how than to do it oneself. E. M. Forster is a master of his material, a master of narrative. Yet even he confesses that "people will not realize how one flounders about."

Floundering about is endemic to writers, a phase we all go through at the outset of a work. Psychiatrists say this initial block is intrinsic to the creative process, a forcing of the writer deeper into himself. The procedure can be called by other names: thinking, brooding, dreaming. I have heard it said that most authors sit down at their typewriters too soon. Before words go on paper the biographer must put his notes away, out of sight, while he sits and thinks, or walks about and thinks — a painful exercise which may consume days or weeks while the paper remains blank in the typewriter.

This thinking may well turn upon the business of what the biography is about; its theme, the axis upon which its wheels may turn. Does the plot concern a happy man, a life fulfilled? It has been said that happiness has no story — which in itself is a challenge and a half. The biographer must write very well indeed to make his happy hero come alive; he has an extra dimen-

9

sion to reach, an eighth hurdle to surmount. Happiness has many definitions. Grief is part of living; *Sturm und Drang* does not necessarily mean unhappiness or unfulfillment.

But how variously lives are arranged! The biographer may choose a hero who began in poverty and climbed, or one born into luxury and place, thence falling or maintaining his position as circumstance and his spirit dictate. And how much objective history will these projected chapters include? It is a vital question. Every biography is of course a "life and times." Yet there are degrees and proportions. The life of a statesman is three-quarters "times"; the life of a painter or composer of music may show a very different mixture and balance. A biographer of Justice Holmes told me solemnly that his ambition was to "show Holmes's influence on the stream of American intellectual consciousness." But how could one aim at such an effect or be sure this intellectual stream existed? Will such a plot carry, is it feasible? A biographer can be too high-toned for his own good.

In the biographies I most admire the story moves forward implacably, inevitably. The reader *believes* in Mary Tudor, Elizabeth the Great, Lord Melbourne, George Sand (*Lélia*), Balzac (*Prometheus*). The reader cannot but believe. There are no awkward hurdles, no holes to fall through. Nothing is stretched too far or condensed to the point of collapse. The narrative — the plot — contains us, we know where we are going.

2.

he shape of a biography

In my experience no part of biographical writing is more difficult than finding the form one's book is to take, its outward shape, the skin in which the "plot" with all its ramifications is to be contained. Biography can take many shapes; for convenience they may be grouped under three general headings: the narrative, the topical, and the essay form. These again have their aspects, offering a wide and dangerous choice; by its shape a biography can stand or fall.

Occasionally a fortunate writer may start out with the exact form in mind that suits his "idea," which in essence means his viewpoint toward his hero or toward some essential part of the hero's life that he wishes to stress. It is more likely however that the form is found by struggle and shift in the early part of work, as the writer digs deeper into his subject. Let us say that two or three years have passed in research, during which the author has spent considerable time in arranging and filing his collected notes — a vital part of the program, when final choice is made of the principal scenes around which his book will be built. All of these activities overlap, there is no drawing a line where one ends and the next begins. But it is during these preliminary times and phases that the writer begins to catch a glimpse of the overall shape into which the historical material will fit. Through the murk of disparate facts the light begins to strike.

It is now that the author decides if his book will be straight narrative, carrying the hero from birth to death as do many of the great biographies: Sandburg's Lincoln, Freeman's R. E. Lee, Maurois's Balzac. Or his subject may be treated topically, as indicated by chapter titles: "Hamilton's political science . . . Hamilton's constitutional law and theory." The topical form is well suited to a multiple subject, like Isaac Disraeli's *The Literary Character,* or Stephen Birmingham's *Our Crowd.* Perry Miller in *Jonathan Edwards* attempted a combination of methods. His aim was to write about a man's mind. "The real life of Jonathan Edwards," the Foreword says, "was the life of his mind." The essence of the book therefore is discussed under topical headings; "Revivalism; Naturalism; Sin; The Will." Yet Miller did not like to exclude altogether the circumstances under which the hero's mind developed and functioned. These he dealt with in sections entitled, "The External Biography, I, II, III, IV."

Professor Miller's book is an experiment; whether or not it succeeded is irrelevant here. The point is that a biographer is free to cast about and find the form that suits him. Halfway between the narrative and the topical is "The Hero and . . ." formula. For example, Strachey's *Elizabeth and Essex,* or Neale's *Elizabeth I and Her Parliaments.* This works out well with the multivolumed biography, permitting any number of changes to be rung. Dumas Malone and Claude Bowers use it: *Jefferson and the Rights of Man . . . Jefferson and Hamilton.* The form is especially convenient when a very familiar figure has been chosen; the title makes plain that the author has something new to say about a particular aspect of the subject's life.

The so-called "literary biography," with a writer as hero, is perhaps the best known of the entire genre: witness Maurois's lives of Shelley, Proust, George Sand, Balzac; Marchette Chute's *Shakespeare of London;* Hervey Allen's *Israfel* (Edgar Allan Poe) . Here certain advantages are apparent, such as an articulate hero whose books can be lavishly quoted throughout. Such quotes, if the hero is witty, can carry a biographer over very dusty ground. To write a biography of Charles Lamb, for instance, would be biographer-pie. "How I like to be liked," said Lamb. "And what I *do* to be liked!"

A final type in our category is the essay form, than

which nothing is more delightful to read and more difficult to achieve. On the face of it such a biography swings along free and easy, unpretentious and never clogged with fact. The author can use the first person singular and say outright what he thinks. That enchanting small volume, *Speaking of Jane Austen,* by Sheila Kaye-Smith and G. B. Stern, gives a better picture of the immortal Jane than can be had by reading her full biographies. Margaret Lane's *Purely for Pleasure* has the subtitle *A collection of literary-biographical essays* — and lives up to its promise. Akin to the essay type — call it a bastard cousin — is the biography which is subtitled, *Six Lectures on* . . . Such a book can be excellent, but again it will be bumpy reading if the author is a better speaker than writer and does not appreciate the difference between the two. *Geoffrey Chaucer* by John Livingston Lowes (talks given at Swarthmore College) is an example of how a master does it.

To undertake the biography of a great and famous person is at the same time frightening and inspiring, an awesome confrontation. Perhaps every biographer toys at first with the saving notion that he is merely writing "a book about" George Washington or Sir Walter Ralegh. I myself have scarcely ever begun Chapter One without the solace of deciding that this was not to be a full biography — certainly not a "definitive" one. Merely, I would set down some thought about Tchaikovsky or John Adams or Francis Bacon or Edward Coke and see how they panned out and if some gold remained in the sieve. Agnes Latham's little book on

Ralegh and his poems follows this prescription in her opening sentence — as if she were talking to herself: "It is difficult to believe in Sir Walter Ralegh," after which Miss Latham proceeds to a fifty-page biographical introduction, so intimate yet so authentically researched that we end as wholehearted believers in Sir Walter.

A modest title — *Speaking of Jane Austen* — can be a comfort and even a stimulus to the author. Queen Elizabeth's enchanting tutor, Roger Ascham, said that "A book of lofty title beareth the brag of over-great a promise." The trouble is, one seldom finds a title until the book is done. Many writers keep in mind what they call a working title, too clumsy for a book jacket but helpful in holding the story on the track, within the chosen form. Chapter titles too can serve this purpose, even the overworked "Youth . . . Education . . . Opening of a Career." In Maurois's Balzac these traditional banalities are pleasingly altered to "Apprenticeship of a Genius . . . First Novels and First Love."

Electric circuitry has brought into being a wholly new form of biographical writing, which in the right hands can be brilliantly successful. In *Felix Frankfurter Reminisces,* we have three hundred and one pages of interviews, taped over a period of five years and presented in chronological order, so that a man and his life emerge. Justice Frankfurter was notoriously articulate; he could say anything he had a mind to, whether serious or light, philosophical, legal or juicily malicious, in such fashion that one listens or reads in total fascination. Yet the book owes much to the interviewer, Harlan B. Phillips, who had the imagination and historical training to ask the right questions: "[Mr. Justice] in the report of the President's Mediation Commission you wrote that 'the eight-hour day is an established policy of the country.' . . . in the light of what transpires later in the steel strike of 1919, [this] is worth a word."

"That's worth more than a word," said Justice Frankfurter, and he was off for six pages.

Interviewing is for the biographer so significant a part of his technical equipment and resources that all of us will do well to study Phillips's book, the questions put, the skillful weaving together of material. To refresh Frankfurter's memory, the interviewer used the Justice's papers, his files up to the time he went on the Supreme Court in 1939. By his own admission Phillips soaked himself thoroughly in these papers and in the detail of his subject's past. To the victims of interviewers who have not done their homework — and certainly to all interviewers — Phillips's book stands as a model.

Concerning the finding of a biographical form, my own struggles may be pertinent. Readers perhaps will see no variation in form between one of my books and the next, but to me they fitted into shapes as different as the square and the cone. *Beloved Friend,* for instance, started out as an edition of certain letters between Tchaikovsky and his friend and patron. In the end it became a biography within "The Hero and . . ." formula, subtitled, *The Story of Tchaikowsky and Nadejda von Meck.* A later book, *The Lion and the Throne,* reads as straight narrative biography, but it was not so designed. In my mind as I wrote, law and its history was the hero rather than Edward Coke. This was

to be a book about *treason,* using the great state trials of
seventeenth-century England as illustration. Treason in
relation to the state, the crown, the nation is a subject
pertinent at all times. And if the biographer is to
believe in his work, he must indeed feel its relevance to
his own day and era.

But as the book progressed it became evident that the
clearest and most feasible way for a nonlawyer to write
about treason was to place it in the framework of a life.
So also with the constitutional questions that treason
brought up: the citizen's rights against self-accusation in
court, his privileges and procedures in Parliament under
the law and many such matters. I experimented with
half-a-dozen forms, some of them more fantastic than
Perry Miller's. For instance, I tried typing all the facts
in red ink and all my ideas about the facts in black ink.
In desperation I began again, with Coke's birth, and
carried him along to age fifty without following any
form at all. The material was vast, with great chronological gaps between events, so that writing it down was
like weaving an endless tapestry of courtroom scenes
and legislative chambers, with Coke's face appearing
now and then as a kind of signature.

In the end the records divulged enough personal
material about my hero and his family so that the whole
could be unraveled and rewoven in straight, inclusive
narration. The experience caused me to wonder if other
biographers have equal trouble finding their form, or if
they wake on the seventh morning with the whole
neatly arranged and tabulated. Of one thing I feel sure:
the length and weight of a finished manuscript, the
number of years spent, influence the biographer when

he ends one book and prepares for another. If the last opus was long and consumed six or seven years, then this time, he tells himself — *this* time the book will be short. And it will be light in the hand, something pleasing to read in bed.

Moving from book to book, the biographer needs a change of form, first because the new subject calls for it, and also because repetition stultifies. A writer cannot forever tread the same old road, and the breaking of new paths is exhilarating. For myself the shift from Edward Coke to Francis Bacon, who came next, was like moving from the forest to the plain, though Sir Francis too presented his difficulties. Being a man of worldwide fame he must be approached very differently from the almost forgotten Sir Edward. Bacon's fame indeed could determine the book's shape; one need not include everything, explain everything, but could assume the reader knew the outlines. One might proceed as if one had already written a biography of Sir Francis and this book was an afterthought, conceived in the essay form but chronological, with the man's life etched in as a base and framework. Perhaps (one thought) it would be well to write the whole thing as lectures? I went about procuring six lectures at a university: "Francis Bacon," they were called. Then I wrote the six and delivered them seriatim from a platform — and thought my work was done.

But the lectures, when read in sequence and in solitude, would not do in book form. So I put them aside and began again. This time the material proved manageable, reduced as it was to smaller dimensions. Men's lives seem to divide, for narrative purposes, into three parts, as earlier indicated: youth (family background and education) ; career (the rise to fame) ; old age and death. Bacon's extraordinarily active life fell of itself into a drama of five acts, distinct from one another, with a curtain drop between. Each act had its title page: (I) An Elizabethan Eden. 1561–1579. (II) The struggle to rise. 1579–1613. (III) Bacon ascending. A time of glory. 1613–1620. (IV) Impeachment. 1621. (V) A noble five years. 1621–1626. This design grew out of historical material which permitted Bacon's story to start slowly, in an Eden of childhood innocence and happy surroundings, then mount through heartbreaking struggle to a pinnacle of worldly achievement (the lord chancellorship) , meet with the climax of sudden fearful humiliation (impeachment and conviction) , and at the end (V) taper off into the period Bacon's friends called the *nobile quinquennium.*

To define these differences in form is difficult. All one can do is give examples as illustration of an author's casting about, the trial and error that go into the making of a book. Actually the thing is evanescent, clear only to the biographer and at times far from clear even to him. *Francis Bacon, The Temper of a Man,* is the only one of my biographies that I can pick up and read without discomfort. An easy, discursive shape gives latitude. In spite of brevity one could say what one thought, using, though sparely, the first person singular. Moreover one could confess there were things one did not know and must leave to the reader's judgment, such as the question of Bacon's moral guilt in the bribery charges; legally his guilt was indisputable.

3.

he opening scene

Where should a biography begin, with what scene shall it open? If the hero's name is famous it can open with his birth. The reader will be interested — for instance — in all there is to know about Sir Isaac Newton and will relish what the midwife said about his being too puny a babe to live, or how as a schoolboy he bought ale and cherries and then listed them in a notebook as *"otiose and frustra expensa."* On the other hand a life of our Indian agent on the frontier, Captain B ——, had best open with a battle or a skirmish — some scene to catch the reader's attention, show that the hero and his doings are important and exciting and perhaps have a bearing upon history. Once that is established, the writer can turn back, flash back to the youth-and-education chapters.

The business of deciding at what age the hero shall be introduced is vital, intrinsic indeed to a biography's entire structure and may well have been decided early in research. Or it can be determined on the spot by trial and error. Two of my biographies opened with the birth of the hero. One of them opened when the hero was two, one when he was twenty-six. Another began seven chapters and forty-one years before the subject, Oliver Wendell Holmes, Junior, was born. And one, *Francis Bacon,* opened with a sixteen-page prologue entitled "Lord Bacon's Reputation," aimed as reminder of a subject, a person, whose name we know well but about whose character and actual life we are hazy.

Much skill can go into an opening sentence or paragraph, and to my mind the result is worth any amount of trouble and revision:

> When Henry VIII died in January 1547, the most remarkable beings left in the realm were three pale and close-lipped children. One was his daughter Elizabeth by his second wife Ann Boleyn . . .

That first sentence of Miss Jenkins's includes everything: dates, names, places — "the realm" could only be England — and the moving description of three pale and close-lipped children. No footnote is needed to establish these identities, nor do we require the tedious genealogy with which biographies are prone to open. For myself I cannot read such paragraphs or pages. Surely they are material for a writer's first draft, and can be incorporated piece by piece later on, inconspicuously.

An inspired opening of another kind comes from Mattingly's *The Armada:*

> Mr. Beale had not brought the warrant until Sunday evening but by Wednesday morning, before dawn outlined its high windows, the great hall at Fotheringhay was ready.

We are going to have the execution of Mary Queen of Scots and no reader can resist; one would rather go without dinner or stay home from the party. The scene does more than attract by sheer drama. It is a logical lead into the Catholic question — a problem political as well as religious, involving Spain, France, Rome, all Europe, and at home in England the focus of dangerous disturbance.

Contrast a less successful opening of the same descriptive kind, set in the same period:

> The clangour of mailed footsteps, sounding like a storm of hail in the passages of the Tower of London, died away; and now a black frost of silence sealed the world from all life.
> The outer world seemed dead.

Thus Edith Sitwell opens *The Queens and the Hive,* her biography of three English sovereigns. When I read this I did not believe a word of it. Here is make-believe which reads like an old E. Phillips Oppenheim novel. "The outer world seemed dead." Dead to whom, pray? The word *seemed* is a trap for biographers; Miss Sitwell, a splendid poet, should have known better. Yet how natural if Miss Sitwell told herself that after poetry, biography would be easy. No shape to it, no rigorous confines and counting of syllables. One could simply roar off and let the words fall where they would.

Miss Sitwell's opening sets the tone, true enough. Her book is a period piece, loud with mailed feet and the whisper of treasonable conspirators. But the biographer can sacrifice too much to tone. For myself I prefer a quieter opening unless, like Mattingly, the author uses bare facts for his dramatic effects. But using bare facts presupposes a truly formidable knowledge of history. To choose exactly the right facts, pertinent and telling, one must have in mind *all* the facts. Senator Albert Beveridge wrote a four-volume life of Chief Justice John Marshall, who was born in 1755. The book opens with a cry, an alarm: "The British are beaten! The British are beaten!" In a moment, after the first shock of surprise and identification, the reader is back there with Braddock in the Allegheny wilderness, where Beveridge wants him to be. 1755 — and France, not England, is the enemy. We are not yet "Americans," we are Britons and proud of it. Beveridge's opening rings in the ear, reminding us there was a time when we cared if the British were beaten; their defeat was ours. *The mother country, our friend and our protector.* In any book about the American Revolution it is well to start out by establishing this relationship, not merely as fact but as emotion. The reader should feel it, as Keats would say, upon his pulses.

Mrs. Abigail Adams Homans wrote, at eighty-odd, a little book about her life in the celebrated Adams family. It is entitled *Education by Uncles.* "When I speak of my background," writes Mrs. Homans, "I am speaking of something that is dead as the dodo." What a lovely beginning! Not only is the tone set — a blithe chiding of revered names, of sacred Boston cows — but the words sound like the author's own speech, terse, humorous, unexpected. One need not have met Mrs. Homans to recognize this. It is a great thing to live long enough to be oneself, an even greater thing perhaps to be able to write prose that "sounds like the author." Few achieve it, very likely few even think about achieving it.

David Cecil opens his *The Young Melbourne* with a chapter entitled "Prologue: The World." The first sentence is rather pedestrian: "The great Whig country houses of the eighteenth and early nineteenth centuries are among the most conspicuous monuments of English history." But the ensuing pages set out the scene gloriously, as only a master could do it. We see the great colonnaded entrance halls, the cream and gilt libraries, the deer park beyond long windows — the combination of country ease and magnificence, of pleasant family life and ruthless snobbery that marked an era and a class. Lord David Cecil belongs to that class. Yet because he is an artist he is apart from it and looks at it without envy yet also without mercy. Never was a more fortunate mating of biographer and subject, nor a more felicitous first chapter of a book.

24

The opening scene

Once in a fortunate while the subject, the hero himself, presents the biographer with an incident that estab-
lishes an opening, complete with time and place. When
John Adams was an old man, Dr. Benjamin Rush of
Philadelphia, fellow Revolutionist and longtime friend,
wrote inquiring if Adams recollected when it was he
first became "a politician." Adams replied that he did
indeed remember; it was in the year 1745, when he was
ten years old and New Englandmen took ship for Nova
Scotia to capture Louisbourg from the French. This and
the resultant threat of D'Anville's hostile fleet bearing
down upon Boston, gave the boy his first involvement
with the affairs of his nation.

With such a lead, one's opening pages need only show
these events and their effect upon the Adams family,
living obscurely on their Massachusetts farm. This however was the only time the material so clearly indicated
my beginning. With *Miracle at Philadelphia* it took
three months' unremitting experimentation to find an
opening. A working notebook complains bitterly about
the impossibility of starting this book; one entry even
attempts the comfort of a forlorn jest: "Holmes said,
'Have faith and pursue the unknown end.' I am pur-
suing the unknown beginning."

It has helped me to discover that even the giants
had their troubles at the start. In the Staats Bibliotheke
on Unter den Linden I once sat, by permission of the
curator, with the manuscript of Beethoven's Fifth Symphony on my lap. To my astonishment and awe the
master had written his first two bars — those measures
with the famous rhythm which E. M. Forster identifies
as "dididdy dum" — then slashed his pen through them.

True, the top line was only the flute part but even so it was impressive.

The eighth edition of Clarendon's celebrated *History of the Rebellion* reproduces the manuscript of page one in the author's original version. On the top left-hand corner is enscribed the date when Clarendon began: March 18, 1645. Below, the first paragraph sets off with a rush: "If for no other reason than that posterity may not be deceived by the prosperous wickedness of these times . . ." A black, determined pen has crossed out the first six words so that the sentence reads, as published, "That posterity may not be deceived . . ."

Such tentative beginnings are more comforting than, for instance, the trumpet blast of Macaulay's opening to the five-volume history of his native land: "I purpose to write the History of England from the accession of King James the Second down to a time which is within the memory of men still living." It is typical of Lord Macaulay. What magnificent confidence, what striding ahead with large steps, what triumphant heralding! One may admire, but one would be terrified to meet such a man, on earth or in heaven.

The ordinary workaday writer must be willing to experiment, throw away a page or two, or a chapter. To regard one's every written word as sacred is fatal, yet I have seen more than one author succumb to this fatality. Surely there are ten ways of saying anything, everything. The trick is to find the way best suited to your material and if the best way does not reveal itself, then take the second best. But get on with the story! This — remember — is biography you are writing. You are bound strictly by your historical material. You cannot transcend it, you cannot lean on the wind and float off into poetry and the sweet blue yonder.

College students, after a lecture, have sometimes asked me to describe my failures, my bad tries. It helps, they say, to know the professionals have their troubles, too. By that token it may be pertinent to record one of my most disastrous attempts at beginning a book: *Beloved Friend,* about Tchaikovsky. This proved not a matter of a few false starts but a genuinely wrong slant or direction pursued through a third of the book. The plot, the subject matter, as earlier indicated, was the extraordinary relationship between Tchaikovsky and his patroness, Nadejda von Meck, designed to be written as straight narrative and interspersed lavishly with excerpts from letters. I wrote fifty thousand words and sent them to my critic, who at the moment was most inopportunely away for the summer. (Critics and editors are forever going off, out of reach.) She returned the manuscript with a letter saying she *hated* (in italics) Tchaikovsky and was disappointed in the whole venture. She could not be interested in a young man who took money from a rich widow and then never had the courage to meet her face to face. What a sponge, was he CRAZY?

It was a stunning blow. Fifty thousand words, and wrong? After such criticism the writer — any writer — reacts by anger and a quite furious resentment toward a false friend who views life and letters through lenses plainly opaque. Why not send the manuscript elsewhere, get a second criticism? This fine indignation was followed by depression. Furtive glances at the manuscript showed that it was indeed weak in spots. But what to do? Genius aside, Tchaikovsky was a nice fellow, a

27

charming generous man whom everybody liked. How could I have misrepresented him to such extent?

The trouble was — one began slowly to see it — Tchaikovsky and his lady had been thrown, *à deux*, too suddenly at the reader, who had been asked, all unprepared, to swallow a situation too concentrated for quick digestion. To perceive this error took time, days and weeks which any writer will recognize as uncomfortable, even agonizing. One fine morning I sat down and began the whole story over again, using exactly the same historical material but presenting it differently. The initial scene was retained, where the widow hears Tchaikovsky's music for the first time and is stirred by it. But instead of letting the friendship be established straightaway (which in fact it was), chapters of flashback were interpolated. The first gave Nadejda's background, her sensitivity and genuine emotional needs. Then came Tchaikovsky's background: "If, for Nadejda von Meck the time was ripe for this new friendship, on Tchaikovsky's side the need was no less urgent." It required three full chapters to describe this mutual need, lay out material personal to both characters and also inform readers of the peculiar politico-musical situation of Russia in the 1870's — something highly germane to the plot but which had been skimped in the first writing. Not until Chapter V were the two characters allowed to make their tenuous connection. I typed further into the story and sent it off by mail. My critic wrote back that well, well, she *liked* this man, Tchaikovsky! It was a complex relationship between him and the lady but she understood it now; he'd have been wrecked without the widow's money. . . .

The opening scene

How hard it is to find a shape for one's book, a path to walk upon! One begins that first chapter, that opening sentence, in a fist-clenching mood, a mood of prayer, despair or — rarely — exaltation. There is a wall between me and words — a novelist said it — which keeps me always striving.

4.

he end scene. Burden of the whole

In all this talk of difficulties, of false starts and floundering, let it not be forgotten that form serves the writer, it does not hamper him. Once decided on, the form within which he must move gives the biographer freedom to expand. Discipline opens the door.

A master of plotting and narrative, Somerset Maugham, has said, "It imports us as much to know how great men die as to know how they live. . . . That last inevitable step has a fascination . . . which no previous event can equal." A biography is disappointing if it does not include the death scene. Yet biographers are often guilty of this omission. Failing evidence on which to build a scene, let us at least be told how the hero died, of what disease, did he have a splendid funeral, was he greatly mourned? I remember a biography that went along well enough with the story, carrying us back to the eighteenth century and keeping us there for the hero's lifetime, until suddenly the word *died* appeared on the page, with a date. Printed opposite was a photograph of the hero's grave with a man in a derby hat looking down at it — out of time, out of scene, out of character. To the reader the shock was lethal; then and there the book died with the hero.

A superb death scene occurs in *Elizabeth the Great,* doubly difficult because the historical material has been worked over so often. But Miss Jenkins, reassembling the evidence, has put it together with a directness and withal a splendid historical imagination that lets the scene emerge with startling effect:

> By the end of February [the Queen] was declining fast. It was put about that grief for Essex had deprived her of the wish to live, but as potent a reason was perhaps a perfect sense of timing. She had told the Houses she did not wish to live and reign after her life and reign could do them no good. "She grew worse," said her cousin Robert Carey, "because she would be so." . . . When Carey was admitted to see her, he kissed her hand and said something of being glad to see her better.

She took his hand and wrung it hard and said, "No, Robin, I am not well," and she sighed and sighed as he had never heard her do except when the Queen of Scots was beheaded.

Sighed and sighed. It is a wonderful stroke, almost onomatopoetic; one hears the labored breath as the fading strength ebbs out.

Her symptoms increased, of fever, restlessness, sleeplessness, perpetual thirst and phlegm in the throat. When she was too much exhausted to walk about she sat on the floor-cushions and once there she would not move. Cecil said, "Madame, to content the people you must go to bed." The Queen gave a smile of indescribable scorn. "Little man, little man," she said, "the word *must* is not to be used to princes. If your father had lived ye durst not have said so much."

Twice, the author has cast back to scenes and persons vitally significant to her story: the execution of Mary and the name of the Queen's beloved minister and servant, Lord Burghley. In actuality, when a person dies, the family, the watchers habitually cast back, mourn the past, recall this incident and that as if to hold off the imminent terrible future.

At the end of the fourth day [the Queen] was so faint they were able to carry her to bed. . . . Midnight came and then it was March 24, the Eve of the Feast of the Annunciation of the Blessed Virgin. At a quarter-to-three the watchers again approached the great bed.

Elizabeth was lying with her head on her right arm. Her warfare was accomplished.

Sometimes luck favors the biographer. Glorianna, the Virgin Queen, need not have died on the Eve of the Feast of the Annunciation. On the other hand nothing is more baffling for the biographer than to reach that last climactic scene and not have historical evidence to permit the proper telling of it. Sir Edward Coke, for instance, died at Stoke House in Buckinghamshire when he was eighty-three. His last years had been peaceful, resigned, there was reason to believe he died quietly. One thought of one's own father at eighty-six, saying easily, "I will find out what is on the other side." Edward Coke, the old fighter, seemed ready to go. But I had at hand no real evidence to prove it. In a last desperate search of the printed records a note emerged, written by a contemporary: "Died at his house at Stoke," it said, "mine old friend and fellow Bencher, Sir Edward Coke, Knt., being Wednesday between eleven and twelve of the clock at night, in his bed, quietly, like a lamb, without any groans or outward signs of sickness, but only spent by age."

Now, how could that note have been overlooked for five mortal years of reading? The records in England and at home of course contained it. The man who wrote the note, a Master of the Rolls in Chancery, often entered Coke's story; he bore the unforgettable name of Sir Julius Caesar. Never mind, the scene was made, the biographer's guess had been right.

33

There can indeed be something characteristic, revealing, in the way a man dies; his end seems to match his beginning, he dies as he has lived. The poet Shelley died young, drowned in the sea off the coast of Italy, where he was sailing for pleasure. Is there not something fitting, inevitable, in the vision of that small boat, that windy summer sea? Is it not an essential part of a life passionate and inspired, and can one imagine Shelley *old?* There are men who cannot, must not age; it has been said a cavalier is always young. On the other hand Robert Frost's old age is intrinsic to him and to his poetry. The witty, clipped lines of verse were part of the Frost legend long before he died.

In earlier centuries, when mankind professed to endure a life on earth merely for the sake of heaven and a hereafter, what one died of was far less important than the person's spiritual condition at the final moment. "My Lady Haddington died wonderful religious and most well prepared for heaven." Tracts were circulated on how to die, how to take one's departure in a manner to ensure reception at the other end. *De Arte Moriendi,* the *Booke of the Craft of Dying:* it was a current and timely subject. Today's public still shows avid interest in a man's final words. "This is the last of earth! I am content," said old John Quincy Adams. "Let us cross the river," said Stonewall Jackson, "and rest in the shade." The words are part of our American tradition.

The end of a biography is difficult, and the difficulty starts about two thirds of the way through. With dismay the biographer realizes how much has been left unsaid; as an old writer put it, "Matter multiplieth toward the conclusion." How can all this material be squeezed in at this late date? The answer is, it cannot. Unless a man has met with a violent end, his life does not become crowded in old age; it tapers off. The reader should see this tapering off, be aware of it, aware of the hero's narrowing circle and sometimes of his deepening wisdom. It is no accident of liturgical music that after the crucifixion comes the benedictus.

Suppose your biographical hero is introduced at age ten and lives to be ninety-odd? The reader should see him and know him young, mature, middle-aged, old. "To live over people's lives is nothing," said Henry James, "unless we live over their perceptions, live over the growth, the change, the varying intensity of the same — since it was by these things they themselves lived." The reader should see the hero growing old, changing from chapter to chapter. This is one of the hardest tasks in biographical writing. Sometimes I wonder if the difficulty lies within the biographer, who himself does not like to think about growing old. Of my own biographical heroes it happens that none was cut off in his prime; all of them lived to be much older than the author at the time of writing. Consequently the evidence lay outside, in observation, and one went about observing men of fifty, sixty, seventy, eighty, ninety. How did they walk? And when they had been sitting, how did they rise — with their hands pushing down on the chair arms, or with a cane leaning ready? One looked into the faces of the old, one studied Holbein faces, Dürer hands, Rembrandt brows, the rheumy eyes, the gaping mouths. How ruthless these great painters! They could look at anything, portray anything; they had braved the fact of their own mortality, met it head on and hard-eyed.

The biographical words "he died" by no means succeed in killing off the hero. Death is indeed a hard fact to credit. I heard a physician say that no matter how many deathbeds he attended, he felt always a shock of disbelief when a man stopped breathing, particularly a young man. "It is incredible that his chest doesn't move." Readers too must believe in the hero's death upon the page. And before this can happen the biographer must himself believe in it. Merely because a writer is anxious to end his book does not mean he enjoys killing off his subject; I know from experience. Three to six years in a man's company disposes toward friendship, makes for a dependence that is very real. Parting is uncomfortable and the writer feels restless, though once the thing is accomplished and the cord cut a kind of oblivion descends; the biographer feels as if somebody else had written his book. In describing an old person's death it is especially helpful if the writer casts back, as Miss Jenkins with Elizabeth, recalling this life in all its weight and balance, its heroism and ultimate significance. Nostalgia enters in, and sadness. The reader needs preparation for that shock, that ceasing of the breath.

In his excellent book *Art as Experience,* John Dewey speaks somewhere of the artist's spiritual burden during a long book — the burden of keeping in mind at all times one's entire story: the beginning, the middle and the end. We might call it the burden of the whole. From the opening page the biographer should bear in mind the end of the story, feel his face turned toward it, his plot moving toward it as inevitably as the Olympic runner moves toward the finishing tape. J. P. Marquand said that "one of the best novelists who is writing today once told me that he is always thinking of his final scene down to the last words before *'finis'* is written, through all the months during which he may be drafting his story." For the biographer this principle applies whether or not the narrative ends with the hero's death. Perhaps the book stops much earlier, with some triumphant incident of the hero's youth, some tragedy of his middle years. At any rate the story should swing full circle. Chapter 32, let us say, should be not merely Chapter 32, but the last chapter, the end.

A significant or dramatic ending to a life makes the subject tempting to biographers. The plot, the drama is before you on the road, you need only follow to that final act. In such cases I could imagine composing the death scene first and then going back — a daring procedure; I for one have always composed in strict chronology, one scene leading inevitably to another. Yet such a plot is a perfect example of what Marquand meant: writing of Charles I of England or Mary Queen of Scots or Sir Walter Ralegh, the biographer must be constantly aware of the scaffold and of his subject's manner of meeting violent death. On the first page the book should foreshadow this ending. In short, the end must match the beginning, else the reader feels cheated, unconvinced. He does not believe what he reads even if every word has been factually correct and the author's five-by-eight research cards have never lied. In the case of Ralegh especially, who died at sixty-three, it requires an entire book rightly to explain how and why an English hero was sentenced to a traitor's death.

On the other hand, as has been said, a long life followed by a natural death is a factor which basically affects the shape of a biography. This is not to imply that a long life necessarily calls for a long book. What it does is to determine the writer's direction and the pace at which he lets his story move. With Adams, who died at ninety-three, I made an all but fatal mistake in planning. Perhaps it is worth reporting if only as an object lesson.

"Thomas Jefferson survives." These were Adams's last words, as he lay dying in Quincy, Massachusetts, on July 4, 1826, the fiftieth anniversary of Independence. Unknown to Adams, Thomas Jefferson died on that same day in Virginia. This double departure of the heroes was epic, tremendous, and needed only to be set down in its bare facts. How could a biographer miss, I asked myself, and looked forward with relish from the day Adams was chosen as subject.

Yet because I did not keep in mind proportion, because I let myself be carried away as the material expanded, I forfeited my scene altogether, and by some fifty years' chronology. By the time 1776 arrived, my quota of words was spent. Already the manuscript was book length, though Adams was not to be elected President till 1796 and his death was half a century away. I went over the manuscript, trying to cut. But deletion reduced this rich life to mere annals, a list of events; the blood ran out of it with cutting. The book would have to stop in 1776, be chopped off ruthlessly — and there was to be no second volume.

History came to at least a partial rescue. The Declaration of Independence marked the end of an empire. The Fourth of July, 1776, was therefore a death and a rebirth, the very Easter of our national spirit, and I said so. But even as I wrote the lines I felt cheated. Nothing could substitute for that other, grander scene, lost to the biographer forever because she had forgotten her plot and its proportions.

5.

 he biographer's relationship with
his hero

"One should write only about what one loves." ("*On ne doit pas écrire que de ce qu'on aime.*") Renan, the biographer and historian, said it in the last century and for this writer at least it is profoundly true, the more impressive because in Renan's lifetime he withstood prolonged literary attacks. If so tough fibered an author confessed that he loved his subjects, why might not the rest of us do the same? For a considerable time it was unfashionable to admire one's biographical hero; the debunking period lasted a full generation. Lytton Strachey started it and on the whole it was a healthy movement, a reaction against the laudatory familial biography of the nineteenth century. But Strachey was a brilliantly talented writer; his imitators and followers had not his genius and the art of biography suffered. We outgrew the fashion, perhaps because debunking is easy and what is too easy does not hold up. Trollope said, "There is no way of writing well and also of writing easily." But the stigma remained; a book was not true unless it was malicious.

After the debunking era, biography went through no more literary fashions. Indeed, to the general surprise it has become immensely popular. One of the advantages of being a biographer is this freedom from changing literary modes. People want to read the authentic record of other people's lives and they do not want the story clothed in fashionable obscurity, imagery, symbolism. The modern biographer, if he chooses, can write as John Aubrey wrote two centuries ago in *Brief Lives,* or as Isaac Disraeli wrote in *The Literary Character,* or *The History of Men of Genius* — provided the modern writer is equally talented. He can use facts, dates, explanatory parentheses. He can proceed from point to point, from incident to incident with no apology for being old-fashioned, outmoded. Punctuation too is a matter of choice. The biographer can sprinkle the page with commas or, if his ear for rhythm is keen and his sentence structure is firm he can arrange his punctuation as he pleases. Best of all, the biographer is not required to declare that life is a cruel and total absurdity, nor to follow his hero inevitably downhill to drugs, casual sex and a drearily inconspicuous suicide.

This is not to imply that the biographer invariably approaches his work with love in his heart. There are many considerations besides love that may give the biographer his initial inspiration. I asked Miss Prescott in England why she chose Queen Mary Tudor to write about. No subject could be more difficult. In that ill-starred life tragedy followed tragedy; Mary's life was one long defeat. She loved her Spanish husband and was not beloved; she yearned for children to the point of imagining herself pregnant; her deepest instincts were denied outlet and she ended by earning in history the epithet of Bloody Mary. Miss Prescott looked me full in the eye and said, "I chose Mary Tudor because I thought she would make money for me."

One thinks of the traditional advice given the girl about to choose a husband: "Money first, love will follow." Surely it had been that way with Miss Prescott; a tragic story has not been more compassionately told. But it is indeed true that the biographer does not fall in love with his hero at first sight and remain infatuated. Love comes slowly, after deep acquaintance and many arguments back and forth, though one can judge this only by one's own experience. With Edward Coke, for instance, I had a struggle that could have ended in divorce. Here was a brave man, chosen to illustrate a historical point. But he was also stubborn, vain, disagreeable and capable of cruelty. Contemporaries feared Mr. Attorney General; he earned widespread hatred for his bitter, relentless invective as prosecutor. At Ralegh's trial Coke behaved shamefully. Was this, one asked, the

way our freedoms came to pass — in reverse as it were?
Strange, that social progress can be achieved through an
instrument so far from perfect! My workbook argued
the point. "Coke was brutal beyond any excuse. Must I
love him, must I even *like* him?" "No!" I wrote. "But I
must be engaged with him, married to him, at one with
him yet independent, rearing back to look at him."

Looking back, it seems naïve; one forgets the deep
involvement that comes with a five- or six-year book. As
a definition of marriage proper, what the workbook said
would not do. But as definition of biographical marriage
it is valid enough. Perhaps what the biographer needs is
not love so much as identification with the hero.
Whether or no one likes one's subject, it would be fatal
to choose a hero with whom one could not identify.
"Relate" is the current psychiatric phrase. A biographer
can relate to the most diverse and seemingly unsympathetic characters. Something in the subject's life has
touched the biographer's own experience, even though
the deed came no closer than a wish.

Biographers approach their books at certain stressful
periods in their lives. (The lives of artists are bound to
be stressful, without stress they would feel themselves
lapsing unconscious.) Tchaikovsky went through his
days in a state of neurotic anxiety that at times bordered
on madness. "Fear and I were born twins," said Thomas
Hobbes, in one of the more surprising confessions of
history. Perhaps fear, like neurotic anxiety, is to some
natures a necessary stimulus. I think no one could write
these lives who had not experienced neurotic fear, just
as one could not write of Disraeli if he had not felt
ambition, or of Balzac if he did not himself know the

43

furor scribendi. "The need to express oneself in writing," said Maurois, "springs from a maladjustment to life, or from an inner conflict, which the adolescent (or the grown man) cannot resolve in action."

Maurois goes on to confess that he wrote his first biography, *Ariel: The Life of Shelley,* "because it was an expression of one of my conflicts. Shelley had come from a family from which he wanted to escape, and so did I. The problem of Shelley was also my problem. My personality was also expressed in *Disraeli.* He was Jewish. I was Jewish myself. He was for me an example of how to get on with a Christian society. Proust, Chateaubriand and Balzac I did because I admired them as writers. The choices were guided by my inner feelings, whether I can get on with this man or this woman. I couldn't accept the idea of spending three years of my life with someone I didn't like."

On the other hand the biographer is himself puzzled at how completely he can identify with diverse and seemingly unsympathetic characters. The surprise comes later, when he reads his published work. While he is writing he is too absorbed to be thinking about such things as identification. When the biographer has chosen his subject and sits down to read, what he is actually doing for the first three or four months is to make the acquaintance of his hero. Everything comes as grist to this mill: time, place, climate; the hero's friends, his enemies, his appetites physical and spiritual. Any least word about the hero's appearance, how he looked and dressed, is cherished as a lover cherishes the most fugitive news of his beloved. There is a musical comedy song which perfectly expresses the biographer's condition at this stage. Sitting in the research library the tune goes through his head: "Getting to *know* you,/Getting to know all *about* you . . ."

Yet one can be deceived, at first reading and first study. It may indeed be years before biographer and hero come to terms; it is extraordinary how the material can lead astray. Theodor Reik, in his book, *Listening with the Third Ear,* has told how Lytton Strachey changed his mind about Queen Victoria while he was writing her biography:

> Studying the early life of the young Queen, [Strachey] did not like her very much. He saw her as a spoiled, overly self-assured and level-headed girl. He treated her at first with a certain ironical remoteness and with little sympathy. The more he studied her life and the more he began to understand her personality and the environment that helped form it the more sympathetic he became. At the end, when he speaks of the Queen in her last years, you feel genuine human warmth, appreciation, and admiration for an impressive personality. He started with little affection for his subject, and ended practically in love with the old lady.

With Sir Francis Bacon I had something of the same experience. I began his biography influenced by immediately previous years of reading for the life of Sir Edward Coke, who was Bacon's bitter rival both in the law courts and privately. Alexander Pope had called Bacon the wisest, brightest, meanest of mankind and I was inclined to agree. But when I began to study Bacon's works and his career more deeply I recognized my bias and saw that my hero's fall from high estate was no matter of smallness or meanness but tragedy in the grand manner, to be approached not with condemnation but with awe. In the end a biography that had begun in doubt finished on a note of solemn celebration.

A biographer's relationship with his hero can operate two ways. Sometimes the subject takes over, the author merely follows along. With Francis Bacon one was writing about genius. And when one does that, it is the genius that makes the rules. "In many instances," says Maurois, "it is a question whether the man we study was a really great man or a rather base character. The biographer has to choose. He cannot write a complete life of a man without deciding whether he likes him or not, whether he trusts him or not. Of course he may decide that, like most human beings, his hero was a mixture of greatness and weaknesses, but that also is an interpretation."

Even the biographical scene — the time and the place — can enlarge a writer's horizon. One has sat in the Long Parliament with Cromwell, or at the Constitutional Convention with Madison and Washington. One has walked the London streets in a plague year and has seen doors black-lettered in the houses of the sick: *Lord have mercy on us.*

Is all this to have no influence, leave no scar? Can the author put it from him only by writing *finis* to a book? Even dreams leave their residue; a day, a week can be colored by a fleeting picture seen in sleep. As to the effect a biographer's hero can have upon him, there is no way of overemphasizing it. To spend three years or five with a truly great man, reading what he said and wrote, observing him as he errs, stumbles, falls and rises again; to watch his talent grow if he is an artist, his wisdom develop if he is a statesman — this cannot but seize upon a writer, one might almost say transform him. When the book is done the author returns to the outer world, but actually he will not be the same again. The ferment of genius, Holmes said, is quickly imparted, and when a man is great he makes others believe in greatness. By that token one's life is altered. One has climbed a hill, looked out and over, and the valley of one's own condition will be forever greener.

6.

hat the reader must know

Every historian or biographer, beginning to read for a new book, pursues his own method. There is no surefire way. What one reads will depend upon what one is looking for, what one hopes to find — in short, upon the aim of one's projected book. The biographer's aim I take it is evocation. He wishes to recall, bring to life, persons and times long vanished. He has a conception of his hero which he desires to share; he cannot bear that this man should be forgotten or exist only in dry eulogy or brief paragraphs of the history textbooks. My own prefaces are apt to declare this ambition, confess that the facts on which my narrative is based are available to everyone and that I aim "not to startle with new material but to persuade with old."

This is not the aim of the Ph.D. student who writes his thesis, nor of the college instructor who hopes through his book to win an assistant professorship — the "publish or perish" syndrome. In such case brand-new material must be unearthed, no matter how obscure the subject; moreover, what is presented will be far more important than how it is presented. The biographer goes to his reading and his travels in an altogether different spirit than the academic historian — not a better spirit or a worse; merely, a different one. The biographer searches for news of his hero and for every attending circumstance that will contribute to or enlighten this news, no matter if it be in print or manuscript. Only its pertinence is important. I look on the biographer as a historical journalist and I do not thereby denigrate the art or the craft. On the contrary, such journalism is extremely difficult to achieve both from the artist's and the scholar's angle. "We see many things in rolls," said a parliamentarian in Coke's time, "but we know not with what passion and earnestness it was done."

The passion and earnestness can be realized only by readers who comprehend fully the attending circumstance. If a modern journalist reports, for instance, a Presidential address to Congress, he must indicate the Congressional audience, which Representatives will approve, which Senators will be likely to hurry into committee and crush the Presidential plans. So also with the historian who presents, say, Edmund Randolph's speech to the Constitutional Convention of 1787, demanding a national government that will consist of "a supreme legislative, executive and judicial," rather than a union of the states "merely federal." Why were the words *national* and *supreme* so terrifying to the small states, bringing an ominous silence to the room? The explanation involves local *mores,* state traditions, old fears and old ambitions, names of patriots active in 1775 and names newly risen. This is, indeed, the heart of the story and readers must be informed or the narrative cannot proceed.

It is cautionary to maintain, during the writer's reading and writing periods, a file entitled "What the reader must know." What the reader must know before he can fully savor Ralegh's trial for treason in 1603, or Alexander Hamilton's fatal meeting with Burr on the heights of Weehawken two centuries later. In the finished book the necessary information will be inserted just before the scene opens, so the reader may be conversant with names and events which the biographer had no time to tell earlier, or which were pertinent only to this particular chapter. Readers love a dramatic scene and are therefore willing to be informed; they know a story is coming soon. In such cases it is even possible to introduce in no more than a word or brief paragraph, new characters, complete strangers. Whereas ordinarily the reader balks at a new name, wonders if he has forgotten something and should look back.

A biography is not an encyclopedia, it is the story of a

life. George Macaulay Trevelyan has said it is in narrative that modern historical writing is weakest. I think
this happens when the writer tries to crowd too much
information on his page at one time, or, sinning in the
opposite direction, assumes the reader is familiar with
names and events simply because he, the writer, knows
them so well. All this information, gathered in the
library, has its place, a canny page or paragraph where it
will fit painlessly — which means clearly and entertain-
ingly, so that the reader will feel he has made a discov-
ery. He will say it is amazing that they had no rules of
evidence in early treason trials, and that Ralegh stood
up in the prisoner's box and pleaded in his own defense.
The biographer may congratulate himself if, after publication, hortatory letters arrive, explaining his own
informative paragraphs, as though the information had
come from somewhere else. (I confess to great pleasure
when readers inquire if I realize how shocking it was
that lawyers accepted hearsay evidence in treason trials
of Coke's day, or whether I fully appreciate how diverse
were the interests of North and South when the Constitutional Convention met in 1787.)

Original material, written in the hero's own day, is,
of course, the evidence upon which the biographer in
the end relies. If he could spend all his time on such
material it would be delightful. But he cannot. The
biographer must know what his colleagues, his own contemporaries have written on the subject. Take the question of "What the reader must know" before the Constitutional Convention met in Philadelphia, 1787. Why
was the Convention called and how necessary was it?
Did it meet to serve the entire country, all thirteen

states, or was it controlled by what today are called special interests? Here the writer finds himself embroiled in a fifty-year-old academic controversy, every word of which is pertinent to his theme and must be considered, even though the biographer has as yet little notion of how he will handle all this on the printed page, how much he will omit, how much must be included. What he does know is that he must make himself familiar with every published book on his subject and as far as possible with published articles. That he may miss one is his private nightmare — perhaps the very monograph which altered a generation's historical thinking, though the reading public has by no means as yet caught up with it.

The biographer cannot of course research more than one historical incident at a time. Later, in the writing period, when he arrives at such an incident he can pause and read intensively. But during his initial reading, say the first year of work, he will skim over the more important incidents, note down where the material can be found — in what book, what nearby library — then study enough for his own comprehension (actual presentation will need much more) and press ahead. When one builds a cathedral, what one actually does is to dig a hole in the ground. One's care is with the spadework; the masonry and ornamental carving come later. The architect never forgets his grand design, not for a moment does he dare forget it. But because he is a man and not a god he must proceed by inches, as best he can.

Students often ask worriedly if it is necessary to buy books, and whether they should try to start a library of their own on the new biographical subject. Of course, every scholar craves to own books, and by the time one writes one's first full-length biography one is likely to own a modest working library simply because biographers are readers from their youth. The question, I take it, is rather one of expediency. With every biography there are basic books the writer must have continually at hand for reference, to mark with a pencil, cover with marginal comments. It is hopeless to ask a librarian, May I keep this book two years?

If the subject is American, one of the best investments the student can make is the *Dictionary of American Biography.* Like the lover who asks, How did I live before I knew you? — I myself wonder how I managed before the D.A.B. was mine. Bernard De Voto persuaded me to the purchase; he said it was good for reading in bed. The beginner will make his own book lists to match his needs and his purse. But in writing of past centuries it is well to own old dictionaries and at least one book of maps arranged historically. Jacobs's *Law Dictionary,* for instance, told me how the words *assise, gaol delivery, commission of the peace,* were defined in 1743; I did not want to know how they were defined in the 1960's. Such books can be found in the secondhand shops, sometimes for very little money, though they are growing scarcer every day. Writing a biography is so total an effort that one's life actually must be planned around it. I have known more than one history teacher to refuse a lucrative academic appointment because the college in question was too far from the needed historical sources. Obviously, the best place to live is near a great research library. In these days of Xerox and photocopy one need not inevitably go to Europe. Marchette

Chute found most of the material for her *Shakespeare of London* in the New York Public Library and the rest in nearby cities.

For the historian of the American Revolution, Atlantic coast repositories hold the bulk of the material. Between Washington, D.C., and the Huntington Library in California, pickings are scarce unless one is writing of the frontier. Often enough the biographer's place of residence determines his subject. The scholar who lives in Pittsburgh or Detroit has at hand what he needs for a biography of Major Gladwyn or the renegade Simon Girty. When I knew De Voto he lived in Cambridge, Massachusetts. But I think he could not have written *Across the Wide Missouri* had he not been born and bred in territory where, as he liked to say, the average annual rainfall drops below twenty inches — in his case, Ogden, Utah.

For the biographer there are two distinct phases of research: (1) Reading. (2) Traveling about to countries and places where the hero lived and worked. Because I have covered the latter phase elsewhere, I shall not touch upon it here except to stress the sheer fun and excitement of it. The prime example of this kind of exercise is of course Samuel Eliot Morison, who, in preparation for *Admiral of the Ocean Sea,* voyaged by barkentine, sloop and government patrol boat along Columbus's track, using fifteenth-century methods of navigation and making landfall at Trinidad or San Salvador under much the same conditions his hero had experienced. How better could a biographer retrace the route Columbus followed?

When I was in my thirties, a long time ago, I thought that if I had a Ph.D. in history I could do my reading faster. And indeed, perhaps I could have. But what the years have taught me is that haste is the enemy of scholarship. Great libraries do not respond to haste. In 1826, Joseph Hopkinson, speaking to the Law Academy in Philadelphia, cautioned the students against "reading too much and thinking too little." Excellent advice in any century, not only to lawyers but to all who spend their time in libraries. It is the *thinking* that takes time, and should take time. It will not do simply to sit there half anesthetized, copying on five-by-eight cards or marking pages to be Xeroxed. One's imagination should be active; one must be conscious, again and always, of the form and shape of this projected biography. One must have some notion of what the particular line that is being copied will do for a page or chapter. In the evening at home it is well to go over the day's harvest and write on each card why one has copied this bit of information and where it can be used.

Perhaps it is superfluous to add that the biographer should never trust to memory, not even for the big things, let alone the little ones. In Charles Darwin's *Autobiography* there is an extraordinary paragraph where Darwin asks, in effect, how a man of his "moderate abilities" could have made such a mark on his generation. He says it must be partly because, with a memory "extensive, yet hazy," he could, during a work extending over a long period, recall where to search for the one example or authority needed. This of course is genius; it derives from intense and unremitting interest in one's subject, an absorption beyond the range of ordinary minds. I have wished that I could see Lord Macaulay's files, or Edward Gibbon's. Even those prodigious memories must have needed joggings and reminders.

The biographer in the reading and research period hardly knows which is more formidable, too little data or too much. Concerning the too much, one marvels how biographers will manage in the all too munificent future. Think of the mountains of material that are accruing in our national archives! Thomas Jefferson's papers in more than sixty volumes, Benjamin Franklin's in a projected forty-odd, let alone Franklin D. Roosevelt's, President Truman's, Eisenhower's, J. F. Kennedy's and no doubt L. B. Johnson's. Entire libraries have been built to house them. Think of future tape recordings, conversations with the great — not merely a Frankfurter reminiscing within the covers of a reasonably sized book, but rolls and shelves of tape and photo film. Movies! We shall be able to see the hero eating, drinking. The imagination boggles, the tape will stop at nothing.

Even the remote past can overwhelm with its collected evidence. When I began reading for Edward Coke's biography I feared paucity; there might not be enough personal evidence to bring the man alive. I was soon disabused and found myself swamped in material, wondering if it would be possible to master all these names and scenes and incidents before they mastered *me*. Regarding sheer weight of material, the biographer is worse off than the historian because the latter is apt to spend a lifetime in one century and one nation; with each book he writes he is better informed and needs less preliminary reading. Whereas the biographer skips from century to century and clime to clime; one year he writes about King Philip II and the next year about Hadrian. With each book he must begin from zero, simply make his plunge into the library and wait for the air to clear. When one's folder marked "Books to read" reaches alarming proportions it is well to divide the folder into two or three, marked "Books to read immediately" and "Books to read later." Or more succinctly, Folder A Books, B Books and a folder labeled "Look over again before starting to write."

If this seems haphazard, let me repeat that there exists no sure method; the writer must find his own way to exorcise his devils. The trick is to have pencil in hand when reading, or a typewriter if one is in a library where typewriters are in order. For the writer, one of the blissful things about the period between biographies is that he can sit down to read without a pencil, simply and wholly for enjoyment. He can savor every word, or stop and criticize the sentence structure. He is not reading for information, or everlastingly looking for something.

Looking for something, when the exercise stretches over a period of years, is stimulating; it becomes indeed an obsession, a haunt, a way of life, a walled path one travels seemingly forever, with its own sun and shade and moon and stars. Coffee is that cup you drink before you sit down at the morning typewriter, sandwiches are those things you take out of your briefcase on the library steps at noon, dinner with the family is a surcease, but eight to ten P.M. is a good time to go over the next day's reading list or write letters to persons in distant

57

cities asking for interviews. It is small wonder that one's personal correspondence is dated 1768 instead of 1968 and that one's friends say patiently, "Yes, of course, that's fine — but when are you coming *out* of this book?"

 *esearch, its perils and pleasures*

Reading for a biography is a twofold exercise. Much of the work is doubled. First one collects facts of the subject's life and times. Then one goes scouting to ascertain if these recorded facts are true, accurate. Portraits of course are notoriously suspect; even in recognized galleries they can be wrongly labeled. Old encyclopedias and biographical dictionaries had best be checked with later findings. Appleton's *Cyclopedia of American His-*

tory (1894), for instance, gives information about persons overlooked by later compilations and as such is valuable. Yet it contains some forty-seven sketches of men who never existed. The authors were paid by space and made the most of the arrangement — a feat of imagination that I for one find beguiling if dangerous.

But whom can the biographer trust? Matthew Arnold's words come to mind: "That huge Mississippi of falsehood called history." The catalogue of the British Museum Reading Room has a dread phrase; one comes across it written opposite certain material: "Doubtful and supposititious." Fortunately one develops, over the years of work, a sixth sense; familiarity with historical material does it. One loses one's innocence and goes about, healthily suspicious. Every historian realizes that his book will contain errors of fact; it is impossible to assemble so much material without an occasional slip. A historian has said that "only those who have endeavored to throw into a continuous narrative the vast mass of details involved in any one line of historical study, are conscious how easy it is to fall into error." In convivial hours at the Christmas conventions I have heard historians trade these lapses; I have noted also how, in the academic quarterlies, they pounce upon one another: "A brief look at the almanac would have told Dr. Blank that March ——th, 1861, was not a sunny day. It rained." Just after his *Basic History of the United States* was published, Charles Beard told me, in a kind of Beardian glee, that he and his wife had called President James K. Polk "Leonidas" all the way through the book, including the index. "Leonidas was a relative of the President," Beard said.

Crazy things like that can slide through a whole forest of proofreaders, whose eyes would catch a misplaced apostrophe. Simply, they are not looking for whoppers. In short, any writer is a fool who relies on publishers' readers, or who after publication, blames others for his mistakes. Yet the actual fear of error — a wrong date, a misspelled name, a mistake of genealogy — is something to be reckoned with. During writing this can cause severe block; it is, indeed, a bad dream with which the biographer must learn to live. I have known historians who were so terrified of making mistakes they never finished their books; they were forever making revisions.

One has to steel oneself. A published biography is a terrible exposure and the academic field is dark and bloody ground. Scholars exist who, like grenadiers, build their reputation victim by victim. The review pages of the historical quarterlies are perilous reading. I quote a few samples: "There are so many errors of fact and interpretation in this book that only another book would be sufficient to deal with all of them." . . . The expert in any field is apt to scorn a colleague's output simply because it is not the book he himself would have written: "[The book] is readable, factual, even interesting, which is a lot to say for this kind of volume." Sometimes a long, bitter blast relents at the end: "Despite the criticisms that can be leveled against this book, it is worth the time it takes to read it."

Nevertheless, academics can be said to write the most thoughtful reviews published. They do their homework; one never has the feeling the critic has not read the book. I have gone on at some length about this because I am often asked whether the writer learns from reviews of his work and whether he studies unfavorable criticism, takes it to heart and proceeds to conscious improvement.

The answer is, No! he does not. If the review is favorable the author is happy; if unfavorable he tries to forget it as quickly as possible. Criticism to be of value must come before publication, not after. Veteran writers are apt to ignore reviews, refuse to read them altogether. Criticism of published work may be useful to readers and prospective book buyers. To the writer it is about as helpful as the woman who tells her friend, dressed and ready for the party, "But my dear, you should never wear that color green."

For the biographer these doubts and tremors are strongest I think during the research period. The actual performance — the writing — offers, like every art, its legitimate escapes and devices. Suppose a certain remark of the hero's has appeared repeatedly in contemporary evidence, passing from person to person in letters or diaries, beguilingly illustrative of the hero's character. Even so, one cannot wholly credit the source. Justice Holmes's Uncle John, a lovable, wry-spoken creature, took a long time dying. As the family stood around the bed, looking down at an apparent corpse; the nurse said, "I'll just feel his feet. Nobody ever died with their feet warm." Uncle John opened his eyes, remarked clearly, "John Rogers did" — and never spoke again. Rogers, of course, was burned for heresy in the year 1555.

What biographer could resist the story? Shortly before publication a postal card arrived from an old Bostonian, protesting that John Holmes didn't say it. "That was my cousin Sedgwick," the card announced. Correspondence multiplied; those who were not Sedgwicks testified it had indeed been John Holmes. In the end it seemed best to use a variation of the ancient device: *Legend has it.* "Around Cambridge the manner of Uncle John's going became legend." Justice Holmes's famous remark at eighty, when a pretty girl passed by, "Oh, to be seventy again!" — could be traced to so many old gentlemen that when finally I found it attributed to an ancient Roman I omitted it from my book, thereby laying myself open to subsequent letters quoting the remark and asking how I managed to miss such a gem.

A serious threat to the biographer is the appearance, during the research or early writing period, of another book on the same subject. One feels it as an assault; the writer's very being is menaced. He pages over the volume in a mood of savage despair. Is this biographer going to preempt his best stories? The sources are the same as his own. Of what use style, the shape of a book, its "plot," now that this author has stepped upstage? I know of nothing more inducive to writer's block. The only remedy is to proceed, let your anecdotes stand and forget this new threat. Much later, one sees that a footnote or a chapter note will take care of it. When Stanley Pargellis was Director of the Newberry Library in Chicago, he told me the best time to begin a new biography of, say, Thomas Jefferson, is the day after the latest one appears in print. I am not sure I believe this. Yet for the young writer the idea is salutary; implying as it does that the elders too have faced Medusa and lived to tell their tale.

Another difficulty during research is the crusty custodian of family papers who for reasons of his own refuses entrée, a situation every biographer meets sooner or later. De Voto told me he faced it in the Mark Twain papers, Professor Conyers Read met it with the papers of Lord Treasurer Burghley; the Adams papers have not long been available. If possible one waits it out; the nay-sayers are apt to be aged and they drop off. If the biographical hero is recently dead the writer finds another witness or goes deeper into the evidence. Oddly enough one's best scenes can develop from just such roadblocks and prohibitions.

It is natural for families to protect their loved ones. Yet all too often the sentiment is spurious and reveals itself as greed — the request for a percentage of possible profits — or as a kind of silly vanity. Librarians in the genealogical sections suffer much from the species of ancestor worshipper. In the Newberry a librarian told me of his pleasure when a man came looking for ancestors who were rascals. This reader said he was sick of hearing his wife brag about her forebears. To his immense gratification he found an uncle-in-law who had been jailed for horse stealing.

Sir Edward Coke advised the law student to "read no more at any one time than he is able with a delight to bear away." I think Sir Edward was right. To be tired is one thing. Every research reader grows tired and has to keep on, particularly if he is looking for some obscure incident or buried quotation that is hard to find. But being bored is another matter and for the biographer it is dangerous; in such a mood the material may die on his hands. Better to shift temporarily to another avenue of research. The roving reporter in any field must have a sharp eye, an eager nose for news or he will not find it.

Every worker invents his own techniques for warding off fatigue during the research period. Experienced librarians recognize the problem. The Folger Shakespeare Library in Washington opens at nine A.M. By nine-five the scholars are glued to their tables and their books. At eleven-thirty a buzzer sounds. Readers go outside and cross the square to a cafeteria in the Supreme Court building, where they sit at a long table, eat frugally so as not to grow sleepy, and talk to each other briefly about their problems. Then they return to their books until half-past three, when the buzzer sounds again; the scholars troop downstairs for tea and a smoke — twenty minutes out — after which they read until the library closes at five. Hardy souls then cross the street to the Library of Congress which stays open till ten at night.

How much shall the biographer read in preparation, how long shall he keep on — for a year, five years? The answer depends of course on the subject and on whether the biographer has already written a book in the period chosen, and is therefore familiar with the scene and the dramatis personae. Even so it is hard to know when to stop. Writers talk about this. Presenting their outlines they ask anxiously, "Do you think I know enough, am I ready to begin writing?" Nobody can answer the question but themselves. C. V. Wedgwood in her very helpful book, *Truth and Opinion*, quotes an English colleague who gave it as a good rule to go on reading until one hears the people talking.

Oddly enough this can really happen; the voices do begin to speak. Suppose one is working in the Elizabethan period. After a year or two or three the writer is perfectly comfortable with the word *crazy* for *ill:* "I heard the Lord B ——hath been crazy this sennight but is on the recovery." Or the word *discover:* "The lady's face discovered a conscience uneasy." On the back fly-leaves of books one copies phrases: "A very sober and sufficient gentleman . . . a man of pregnant wit . . . a man of softly nature and easy to be abused." The biographer has no intention of using these phrases. But he must become easy with them; above all he must rid himself of the notion that such ways of speaking are "quaint." They were not quaint in the year 1610 and the biographer who so looks on them will never find his road.

What he is trying to do is to get "back there," push aside the dark curtain that shuts away the centuries. "The past is a foreign country," says L. P. Hartley in *The Go-Between:* "they do things differently there." Yet what the biographer looks for is not strangeness, "quaintness," but a sameness with today, something that he — and his readers — can recognize in terms of their own experience. Sixteenth- and seventeenth-century fathers liked to write little treatises of "Advice to a Son"; for the biographer these can be marvelously evocative. To a son about to go abroad on the grand tour, Francis Osborne wrote, "Gallop not through a town, for fear of hurting thyself or others." At once, we recognize that 1600 had its traffic problem and that young men of eighteen were not going to heed it. Osborne advised ordering gloves and doublet from a French tailor, but Spanish perfumers were best.

The biographer needs these intimate touches if he

would avoid the sterile part of antiquity, the worn-out scenery and artifacts of costume novels. When I was writing about Tchaikovsky, my Russian collaborator, a benign, intelligent lady, used to tell me, "We must beware of the samovars and the wolves." Anyone who writes in the American Revolutionary period must beware of the buckled shoes, quill pens and night watchmen calling the hour. With the Elizabethan period one must eschew the fluted ruffs, Spanish galleons, silver armor. *Prithee* and *forsooth* are blots on the biographer's page; they do not carry across the centuries.

Bad theater, in short, can obscure the best of plots. There are historical stereotypes that narrow our vision and constrict the scene. After all, the London of Elizabeth's day was more than Ralegh throwing his cloak over a mud puddle, or the ravens preening on Tower Hill.

8.

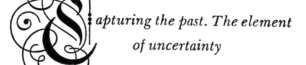

*apturing the past. The element
of uncertainty*

Writing about yesterday, we are conscious of what will follow, we know where yesterday leads. But writing about today we are in the dark. We cannot know, in 1969, what will happen to our country or to ourselves next year, next week, tomorrow. And it is by that hazard we pursue our lives and our circumstances. This game that God invented is indeed so hazardous one marvels men have the strength to play it for a life-span.

In trying to reach that foreign country, the past, let the biographer bear in mind this element of uncertainty in the hero's life or the nation's history. Let him feel it as the awful condition under which mortals move and breathe. Oddly enough biographers forget this, laying down their facts with a kind of smug self-satisfaction, pleased that they know better than the hero. To sustain in his own mind the element of uncertainty is for the writer an act of the imagination and far from easy. To reproduce it on paper means double work. The novelist has only to use his imagination. The biographer too must imagine, but he must present historical evidence, the proper quotation or incident to convince his readers.

In this respect a few facts — quotations from contemporary letters, diaries, news sheets, ballads sold on the street — are for the biographer worth any amount of author speculation of the species that begins, "We can now imagine," or, "It seems probable that." Need I urge the avoidance of an even clumsier way to achieve uncertainty, the coy withholding of a famous name: "A young man, scarcely noticeable, stood in the audience among the groundlings. His name was Will Shakespeare." Writing about Francis Bacon's marriage to a rich alderman's daughter, what was my joy to come upon a letter dispatched quite casually by a London gentleman and dated May 11, 1606: "Sir Francis Bacon was married yesterday to his young wench in Marylebone Chapel. He was clad from top to toe in purple, and hath made himself and his wife such store of fine raiments of cloth of silver and gold that it draws deep into her portion. The dinner was kept at his father-in-law Sir John Pakington's lodging over against the Savoy."

So that is how a great man was looked on by the gossips before the world knew his greatness! Or suppose the hero is a senior at Harvard in the year 1754. New England is concerned because the French have come down from Canada into the Ohio Valley and built a fort named after the new Canadian Governor-General, the Marquis Duquesne. The Boston *Gazette* announces that "several hundred Virginia men" under a young Lieutenant Washington have marched through swamp and wilderness over the mountains and erected a stockade in the Great Meadows below the enemy. Washington has named it Fort Necessity.

The very mistake — "Lieutenant" for Lieutenant-Colonel in the provincial forces — takes us back. Suddenly, Fort Necessity is not a name in a history book, synonymous with defeat, but a desperate small bulwark of defense in the forest. What the *Gazette* has told us makes for recognition of instant danger; we are warm with anticipation. (In music, a like effect is achieved by skillful preparation for return of a familiar theme.) Writing about the making of the United States Constitution in 1787, what I wished was not to have readers exclaim, "How grand a scene and how significant!" — but as the hot summer advanced, to ask anxiously, "Are they going to sign this Constitution, will it go through? Or are these fifty-five delegates simply talking themselves into an impasse?"

While he is reading, the biographer must have a hawk's eye for suitable statements or quotations that will show this fateful uncertainty. Dr. Franklin, in Convention, June twenty-fifth: "In this situation of this Assembly, groping as it were in the dark to find political truth . . ." General Washington, writing from the Convention on July tenth to Alexander Hamilton in New York: "I wish you were back. The crisis is equally important and alarming." There is talk in Philadelphia streets, gossip about how the Convention, meeting behind closed doors, might scandalously vote a king for America. It happens that Christ Church steeple is being taken down, after damage by lightning. A local newspaper, the *Gazetteer,* reports that when the CROWN (in large type) of the steeple came down and bystanders asked what was to be done with it, "an arch boy said they had better wait till the Convention breaks up, and know first what *they* recommended."

Whether or no the reporter invented his little squib does not matter; the effect is there. Mattingly's *The Armada* reproduces superbly this quality of uncertainty, suspense. True, the story of a great battle lends itself to such effect. Yet to sustain expectation is here no easy achievement. The book has thirty-four chapters, the fight does not begin until Chapter XXII, and by then the author has us almost at the breaking point. In Chapter IX, Francis Drake writes to Secretary Walsingham from Cádiz: "I assure your honour the like preparation was never heard of nor known as the King of Spain hath and daily maketh to invade England. . . . Prepare . . . strongly and most by sea! . . . Look well to the coast of Sussex."

One need not be English to feel the threat: Look well to the coast of Sussex! And note the opening to Chapter XV: "As the year 1587 drew to a close, a shudder of apprehension ran across western Europe." If the sentence seems contrived, like a stage direction, Mattingly at once presents the facts to bolster it. In Lisbon, "the least experienced observer could tell that this vast mobilization of ships and seamen, soldiers and cannon was not meant just to protect the commerce of the Indies or stir up trouble in Ireland."

Not content to recite the facts, Mattingly lets us into men's minds through "the least experienced observer." Then, after describing in detail the Spanish preparations, he makes a skillful transition to the general mind of Europe; he gives proof of the mounting apprehension and tells what induced it beyond the incitement of King Philip's armament: "Another cloud lay over the coming year, more mysterious and terrifying than that of war. It had been discerned over a century before, perhaps many centuries before, and as 1588 approached, the awful rumor of disaster spread . . ." Melancthon's fearful prophecy is cited, and that of Regiomontanus before him: there was to be an eclipse of the sun and of the moon. What did it all presage? Surely the end of the world! And the new star in Cassiopeia, omen of disaster on land and sea. Had not Merlin prophesied by his dark science what God in his inscrutable providence was now bringing to light?

Here is no suggestion of "quaintness," nor does the reader say, How foolish and ignorant these superstitions! The paragraphs read as if Mattingly were scared himself. Such is his eloquence that we share the chill and terror of those months.

The mere reading of *The Armada* will not, of course, insure a like success. Moreover the business of looking closely at good examples — the eighteenth century called it emulation — is today outmoded. Young writers are fearful of becoming "typed," as a twenty-year-old novelist told me. I cannot help thinking the danger is remote; no amount of reading *Moby Dick* will make a second or even secondhand Melville. Young writers aspire to "be themselves." Well and good. Yet one's self requires a lifetime to develop. If the writer wishes the image to reach farther than his mirror he can surely benefit from the study and analysis of another man's talent and technical successes.

The element of uncertainty, properly used, brings not only suspense but verisimilitude to the tale the biographer wishes to tell. Uncertainty exists not only in the outcome of a battle, or of a courtship or political intrigue; it is intrinsic to the development of a man's character. What will this boy, this girl, grow up to be — a Cesare Borgia, a Joan of Arc? The public thinks of Lord Melbourne, of Queen Elizabeth, of Sir Walter Ralegh as characters in the round — world figures, themselves confident of their next step. To show them in their hesitant or their stubborn youth requires a subtle use of the new facts at hand. David Cecil does this beautifully with William Lamb, later Lord Melbourne, first describing the boy's happy relationship with his mother — itself surprising in these modern days of powerful devouring matriarchs. At Eton, William has to fight a boy bigger than himself. We have it in the boy's own words. William endures what he calls an amazing pummeling. Then, "I saw I should never beat him; I stood and reflected a little and *thought* to myself and gave it up. I thought it one of the most prudent acts, but it was reckoned very dastardly."

73

The calm good sense of this, the drawing aside to think, even in the heat of combat, was characteristic of Melbourne; already we begin to see the man. Or consider Sir Walter Ralegh, looked on today — especially in America — as a knight *sans peur* and *sans reproche*. Yet it required his trial and execution and his magnificent bearing of this martyrdom to raise his reputation in the eyes of his skeptical countrymen. We know nothing of Ralegh's youth; he is about thirty when the records begin. The point to be made is that in the year 1603, when he was fifty, Ralegh was the most hated man in England. When he was conveyed from London to Winchester for trial, crowds followed the coach, cursing, hurling stones, mud, tobacco pipes. "It is almost incredible," wrote a contemporary, "with what bitter speeches and execrations Ralegh was exclaimed upon . . . It was hob or nob if he would escape alive through such multitudes of unruly people. . . ." Ralegh himself was contemptuous and we love him for it. "Dogs," he said, "do always bark at those they know not."

The problem is to find the reason for this hatred. The records tell us that Sir Walter "was damnable proud . . . and he had that awfulness and ascendancy in his Aspect over other mortalls." We know that the Queen was "taken with his elocution . . . and took him for a kind of oracle, which nettled them all." But what carries conviction are the ballads bought and sung in London streets concerning this arrogant knight, with his money accruing from sweated labor in the Cornwall tin mines:

> *Ralegh doth time bestride,*
> *He sits twixt wind and tide,*

74

> *Yet up hill he cannot ride,*
> *For all his bloody pride.*
> *He seeks taxes in the tin,*
> *He polls the poor to the skin,*
> *Yet he swears 'tis no sin.*
> *Lord for thy pity.*

The biographer of Ralegh could do worse than to open his book with that moment in the coach to Winchester. Here is a Ralegh strange to us, scarcely credible. Elizabeth's favored knight, set upon by enemies now that the great Queen is dead — a character enigmatic, uncertain even at fifty-odd. With such a scene as curtain raiser the writer could proceed to almost any point of the biographical compass: the reader would not lose his bearings, being fixed, rooted, oriented in the drama of Ralegh's plight.

That biographer is fortunate whose hero kept a diary in his youth or whose mother or sweetheart hoarded his letters. To come upon such a treasure trove is a valid reason to choose a biographical subject. Of course a youthful diary may distort the hero's true character; the young are desperately self-conscious, all too apt to "write for posterity." Yet the stiffness and the posturing are themselves revealing to a biographer who possesses compassion or whose own pen in his youth has written the words, Dear Diary. Concerning Trevelyan's remark about how it is in narrative that modern historians fail, I believe the failure comes in this matter of suspense, an overlooking of the uncertainty inherent in both personal and national history. Fiction writers are far more successful in this respect; their craft demands it. Let the

75

biographer then study the best fiction, observe the plot unroll and the hero's character develop from youth to the full majesty of man, or from manhood to defeat as the case may be.

Surely it is no accident that André Maurois, Hilda Prescott, Esther Forbes, Bernard De Voto, John Buchan, Gamaliel Bradford, Bancroft, Motley, Parkman, Henri Troyat, all wrote novels before they wrote biography.

9.

ow men looked: problems of bio-
graphical description

From time to time a book is published that collects
between its covers all the known portraits of a certain
great man — such as Fiske Kimball's *The Life Portraits
of Thomas Jefferson* (1944) or Andrew Oliver's recent
Portraits of John and Abigail Adams (1967). These are
works of highest scholarship and for the biographer,
tremendous time-savers. Tracking down portraits is ex-
pensive and entails travel, besides which the painting in

question is apt to be off somewhere undergoing repairs, or the family is away for the summer and the house closed. For myself, when I have managed to assemble photographs of portraits in printed books which I have bought, I ruthlessly cut them out with a razor and pin them on the wallboard in my study. Constant reminder makes for familiarity. In some families, dominant features repeat themselves down the generations. Even today the Adams nose is strong and prominent, the Adams bald skull magnificent, with a wide, high forehead. To see these traits in living descendants gives validity; my wallboard at one time held thirteen pictures of various Adamses, including John Quincy and a Charles Francis or two.

If the biographical subject is well known, finding how he looked is not too difficult, in spite of wrongly labeled portraits. Portraits failing, one searches for word of mouth, which is often more authentic and certainly more vivid than badly done paintings. To historians of our American Constitutional Convention of 1787 a delegate from Georgia performed an immortal service; William Pierce's descriptions of his colleagues are piquant, believable and not always kind. For Roger Sherman of Connecticut, Pierce's notes bear out the rough but masterly painting by Ralph Earl: "Mr. Sherman exhibits the oddest shaped character I ever remember to have met with. He is un-meaning and unaccountably strange in his manner. But in his train of thinking there is something regular, deep and comprehensive; yet the oddity of his address, the vulgarisms that accompany his public speaking, and that strange New England cant that runs through his public as well as his private speak-

ing make everything that is connected with him grotesque and laughable; and yet he deserves infinite
praise — no man has a better heart or a clearer head
. . . He is an able politician and extremely artful in
accomplishing any particular object; it is remarked that
he seldom fails."

The farther back in time one goes, the more difficult,
of course, to find likenesses. Gazing upon a portrait by
Holbein or Dürer we are convinced that the subject
himself confronts us. But lesser painters arouse our
suspicion. Portraits of Sir Walter Ralegh, for instance,
with ruff and pointed beard, could be almost any Elizabethan courtier. Better to rely on John Aubrey's words:
"He was a tall, handsome and bold man. . . . His
beard turned up naturally. I have heard my cosen Whit-
ney say that he saw him [a prisoner] in the Tower. He
had a velvet cap laced and a rich gowne and trunke-
hose."

Writers in past centuries were nearer the land than
we are today; they used the features of farm animals or
game to describe human beings. This can be confusing.
Both Ralegh and George Washington were said by contemporaries to have "a pig's-eye." What kind of an eye
has a pig? Dr. William Harvey, the anatomist — surely a
trained observer of physical phenomena — said Francis
Bacon possessed "a delicate, lively, hazel eye, like the
eye of a viper." But who has seen a viper's eye, and is its
aspect cold and stony or quick and darting? When I read
this I telephoned the Philadelphia Zoo. The curator of
the reptile house said it must have been a common
English type; Harvey couldn't have seen an African
Gaboon viper. This confused me further, and in the end

Harvey's quotation stood without comment; let readers decide the aspect of a viper's eye.

Collecting details of face and figure is only the first step; the next is to put them on paper. There are many ways to describe a man; the biographer seldom succeeds at first try. Where, for instance, shall a description begin — with the face, the eyes, the manner of walking? With some concealed idiosyncrasy of the subject or with his most noticeable trait, such as a limp, or extraordinary height? "President Johnson is a big man and speaks with a Texas accent." Should one slide into it more subtly, by hint and suggestion? Sir Thomas Browne once wrote that for lasting association he preferred men, "not of retracted looks but who carry their hearts in their faces and need not to be looked upon with perspectives."

We cannot all be Sir Thomas Browne, and a striking description bespeaks a writer of uncommon perception as well as uncommon facility with words. On a printed page the description of a person should conjure up not only the person's appearance, it should suggest the inner man and make good reading. I once heard a girl of twelve announce at family supper the arrival of a new pupil at school: "As soon as I saw Bessie turning cartwheels up the path I knew we were going to be best friends." That was twenty years ago and I have never laid eyes on Bessie. But I know her well.

Thomas Carlyle has a trick of shifting suddenly to the present tense when he launches into a description, especially if he happens to admire the subject: "This man Oliver Cromwell, from Ely, more than any other of these members of the Long Parliament, vibrates my

mind towards him, excites all my curiosity. With what
interest do I see him ambling up at a firm journey-pace
to Town . . . in rude country habiliments, well
wrapped against the cold, — with rugged weather-beaten
countenance! . . . I have marked Mr. Cromwell as a
choleric man; indeed his face speaks it. Look at that
mouth, at those wild deep grey eyes, at that wart on the
brow, at that massive nose; not beautiful, nor yet, in
spite of calumnies, ugly: . . . A troublous dark face,
full of sorrow, full of confused energy and nobleness
. . . Mr. Cromwell, it must be added, is given to weep-
ing: incredible as it may seem . . . For this is withal a
most loving man: who knows what thrillings, wild pangs
of fear and sorrow, burstings of woe and pity, dwell in
such a soul!"

So Carlyle, for three pages of speculation and fact
combined, some of it quite mad sounding, but nonethe-
less vivid and entirely credible. Writers in still earlier
centuries were less turgid but delightfully frank. Even
when we do not know their subjects, the descriptions
catch us up: "Sir John Perrot was a goodly gentleman,
and of the sword. . . . Mr. Caisho Burroughs was one
of the most beautiful men in England, and very valiant,
but very proud and blood-thirsty. . . . [Mr. Andrew
Marvell] was of middling stature, pretty strong set,
roundish faced, cherry cheek't, hazel eye, brown hair.
He was in his conversation very modest, and of very few
words . . . He had not a general acquaintance."

John Aubrey, Sir Robert Naunton, John Clapham —
all of them wrote their brief descriptions before the year
1650. Something original in their minds permitted
them to see with clarity and freshness and to choose out

traits which bring the subjects before us face to face: "He had a very fair clear rosy complexion; a long beard as white as milk, he was tall and slender, a very handsome man. He wore a gown like an artist's gown, with hanging sleeves and a slit; a mighty good man he was." So much for John Dee, Queen Elizabeth's astrologer. After that description, can one ever forget him? In a full biography the writer has the advantage of recurring again and again to his description; on one page giving the face, on another the subject's habit of irony, or the way he eats at table. Such descriptions come through most vividly I think when they stem from love, as Carlyle with Cromwell, or from antipathy, as Carlyle in his description of Lord Bacon at the height of his fame, on the way to be created Baron Verulam: There rides the great Lord Chancellor. "There rides he sublime, with his white ruff, with his fringed velvet cloak and steeple hat and 'liquorish viper eyes.' . . . Undoubtedly a most hot seething, fermenting piece of life . . . made of the finest elements, a beautiful kind of man, if you will; but of the earth, earthy."

Henri Troyat tells how Tolstoi liked to sketch in a character "by beginning with some detail of physiognomy and proceeding by induction from matter to soul, from data to idea. . . . 'For me,' Tolstoi wrote, 'the back is an important mark of physiognomy, and especially the place where the neck joins the back; no other part of the body so clearly reveals lack of self-confidence and false sentiment. . . . A straight back is a sign of passionate temperament. . . . The physiology of wrinkles can be very telling and accurate."

Barbara Tuchman is a master at quick placement and

description. On introducing a new character she easily and painlessly identifies him, then lets us see him: ". . . the post was offered to General Joseph-Jacques-Césaire Joffre, then aged fifty-nine, formerly chief of the Engineer Corps and presently Chief of the Services of the Rear.

"Massive and paunchy in his baggy uniform, with a fleshy face adorned by a heavy, nearly white moustache and busy eyebrows to match, with a clear youthful skin, calm blue eyes and a candid, tranquil gaze, Joffre looked like Santa Claus and gave an impression of benevolence and naïveté — two qualities not noticeably part of his character."

And again, from *The Guns of August:* "Insofar as readiness for war was concerned, the regime was personified by its Minister for War, General Sukhomlinov, an artful, indolent, pleasure-loving, chubby little man in his sixties of whom his colleague, Foreign Minister Sazonov, said, 'It was very difficult to make him work but to get him to tell the truth was well-nigh impossible.' "

A peculiar difficulty comes in describing a very famous man, particularly one who in his country has become a household word. How, for instance, is George Washington to be introduced on the page? Say the time is June, 1787. The Constitutional Convention is meeting at Independence Hall, General Washington presiding, chosen chairman by election. Below him the Pennsylvania delegates sit at their table, among them Gouverneur Morris. To describe Morris is easy, with his peg leg, his heavy, sensual face and worldly manner. But George Washington? Everyone in America has his own vivid notion of that face and figure. To present it is mere repetition, as superfluous as describing Santa Claus. Shall the biographer take Gilbert Stuart's portrait as model and simply reproduce in words the ruddy complexion, the jaw distorted by ill-fitting teeth, the figure splendid, with an effect of majesty?

It will not do. Gilbert Stuart's "Father of His Country" has become a historical cliché, a stereotype. In desperation the biographer asks himself, How did men of the day describe the General's face and figure, before the history textbooks had been written or Parson Weems had embroidered his picture of the riven cherry tree and the boy who could not tell a lie? "His chest is full," wrote an English traveler, "and his limbs, though rather slender, well shaped and muscular. His head is small . . . his eyes are of a light grey color . . . and, in proportion to the length of his face, his nose is long. Mr. Stuart, the eminent portrait painter, told me there are features in his face totally different from those he had observed in any human being. The sockets of his eyes, for instance, are larger than he ever met with before, and the upper part of the nose broader. All his features . . . were indicative of the strongest passions, and had he been born in the forest . . . he would have been the fiercest man among the savage tribes."

What Gilbert Stuart has said reveals almost more than his painting. This happens when we go to source; it is impossible to describe a famous man in any other way. The strongest passions? A man had need of them, to lead a nation through six years of war. One can understand, now, those angry letters to the Congress when supplies failed to reach the Army: "our sick naked, our well naked, our unfortunate men in captivity naked." The Houdon bust at Richmond, seen from a certain angle, reveals another quality not stated in the books — a melancholy, deep and thoughtful. It has been said the people love best those leaders who have sadness in their faces. A young French officer from the Continental Army was in Philadelphia during the Convention; what he wrote home confirms the impression. As Washington emerged from the State House,* "the look on his face," said the officer, "reminded me of its expression during the terrible months we were in Valley Forge Camp."

Certain characteristics of a man long dead are hard to recapture simply because the biographer has not himself seen these traits in actual life and cannot therefore visualize them. A contemporary said that James Madison walked with a bouncing step. This is a peculiarity found in men of nervous energy and strong bodily constitution. I recognized it only because, on a research trip to England, I once followed through Norfolk county a librarian from the Bodleian whose energy was phenomenal and whose shoes apparently contained springs. Plainly, his bouncing was an endowment and stemmed from the spirit, not the instep. Perhaps an ability to describe comes from consciously or unconsciously storing up traits, noting comparisons, types of men and women, so that when a character steps upon the page he will seem credible.

* Independence Hall.

10.

ow men spoke. What they believed.
The biographer's bias

Finding out how one's subjects spoke can be even more
challenging than the matter of their looks. For my part I
cannot write about a man unless the tone of his voice is
plain to me and recognizable. Read until you can hear
them speaking, is indeed a remark with its own overtones. Sir Walter Ralegh's voice was high and surpris-
ingly soft; in Parliament, members called out, asking
him to speak louder. Queen Elizabeth on the other

hand spoke clearly and with so attractive a shaping of her words, an accent so refined that men were ravished by the sound. A Parliamentary reporter confessed himself carried away; he forgot to write and missed the peroration. James Madison was "low-spoken," a trait puzzling in a man who became known as Father of the United States Constitution. Persons of vigor are apt to possess resonant voices. Hesketh Pearson has a detailed and wonderfully effective description of Benjamin Disraeli's voice and manner of delivery in the House of Commons — how he began in a tone "clear but low and monotonous," drawling, using no emphasis, his gestures "calm, untheatrical and uniform." And how, as he prepared to make a point his body became taut, his tone changed, the words were enunciated with extreme care and distinctness, "an icy clarity, an inexorable pungency." The House, electrified, laughed aloud or broke into cheers, Disraeli remaining all the while unsmiling, pale, immobile, "as if he were superior to such human exhibitions . . ."

While studying for *Miracle at Philadelphia* I spent much time trying to find out how my principal characters pronounced their words. New Englanders of 1787 talked through their noses. The Yankee drawl was famous; an English traveler said New Englanders "have a sort of whining cadence which I cannot describe." Dr. Franklin, Boston born, liked the sound. He said the Boston "turn of phrase and even tone of voice and accent in pronunciation, all please, and seem to revive and refresh me." Noah Webster reveals much about local accent. The *Columbian Grammar* (1795) tells even more, with its list of "Improprieties: *acrost, bekays, chimbley, drownded, larnin', ourn, yourn, theirn, watermilyon.*" A man who has been reared in the backwoods never loses his accent; Patrick Henry is quoted as saying that "a man's natteral parts are better than all the larnin' upon earth."

Yet only occasionally and by luck does some contemporary report these accents, or they slip out in the uncertain phonetic spelling of letter writers. How, for instance, did General Washington speak — with the soft Virginia slur of today or with a British accent, derived from his friends and relatives who had been educated abroad? Did Lord Fairfax influence Washington's speech as a youth? Such things can happen. Every society has its plain talkers and its finicky pronouncers, its local accents which can be charming, its Connecticut or Arkansas twang which rasps. In Washington's letters the misspelling tells us little. Some knowledgeable philologist might well make the General's accent the subject of a monograph.

In no shape or form did George Washington's accent come into *Miracle at Philadelphia.* But the biographer lives with his subjects. When Patrick Henry stands upon the public rostrum and holds forth: "I am not a Virginian but an American!" — or even, as in the case of Washington at the Convention, calling the meeting to order — one does not merely see the speaker in the mind's eye, but hears the words emerge and greatly wishes the sound to be authentic. If the biographer in actual life is susceptible to the timbre of a voice, attracted or repelled accordingly, he will be unlikely to choose a subject whose way of speaking is repellent. I myself could not write about Jonathan Edwards, the

New Light philosopher, or even Oliver Cromwell (though I made both attempts) because of the Puritan cant, which comes through the letter books with a self-righteous whine. Writes Cromwell to a friend at the height of his fame, "It's a very vain world. I am not without some assurance that He will enable His poor worm and weak servant to do His will. In this I desire your prayers."

His poor worm? One gags upon the words. This is the same man who reported by letter that "We, after three hours' fight . . . killed and took about 5000. . . . Sir, this is none other but the hand of God; and to Him alone belongs the glory." If this is Christian humility, one understands Nietzsche's repudiation of the meek and suffering Savior.

In skilled biographies there is no jar or jump between an eighteenth-century quoted remark and the writer's ensuing comment. The tone is retained throughout. This is not to say the author affects eighteenth-century prose; that would be ridiculous and next to impossible. But an eighteenth-century quotation is never followed by a twentieth-century idiom. To do so destroys the illusion altogether, brings an air of unreality; we cease to believe what we have read. Our journey is broken; we are no longer "back there," where the author has been at pains to carry us. I have seen this happen more than once, and it derives I think from too rapid composition. The author has not taken time to immerse himself in the period. Style is contagious; a biographer of the seventeenth century will do well to avoid continual reading of careless or journalistic modern writing. If the ear is to become attuned, let it be to the prose rhythms of John Donne or George Herbert rather than the latest popular news columnist.

In *The Young Melbourne,* for instance, the author does not impose on us a single mannered or simpering sentence; his style is free and perfectly natural. Yet his paragraphs fit exquisitely the times and scenes that he describes: "At once gorgeous and dishevelled," writes Cecil, "life at Devonshire House was a continual strain on the spirit . . . the source of its unrest was also the chief secret of its attraction . . . it was quickened by that delicious emotional stir only found in societies whose chief concern is love. It was love that breathed warmth into the social arts in which its inhabitants were so accomplished: love suffused the atmosphere, in which they moved, with a soft enticing shimmer of romantic sentiment and voluptuous grace."

In his file cabinet the biographer's folders on "How they spoke" should rest next to the folders entitled *Customs of the time* — what they ate, how they dressed: costumes of seventeenth-century judges in the high court and the low; the dress of court attendants — filacers and prothonotaries and clerks. And in 1787, did the Philadelphia City Cavalry sport those huge bearskin hats when they rode out to welcome General Washington? . . . No, they did not; they wore round black hats bound with silver. And next to the file marked "Customs of the time" sit the big, full folders entitled, "What they believed."

What they believed is basic, the foundation on which one's narrative rests. Here is the climate of opinion, the philosophic stage-set, within the limits of which the hero must move. Again, Mattingly is superb in this. Telling of men's fears in the pre-Armada year, 1587, he neither condescends from the superior knowledge of the twentieth century (an exercise which academics call *presentism*) nor does he attempt the hopeless task of sharing sixteenth-century beliefs. Chapter XV of *The Armada* is immensely learned, romping through astrology, Scriptural prophecy, numerology and permutations of the number ten without the slightest hint of showing off; not once does Mattingly assume the magisterial tone.

All through the book, Mattingly retains his air of banter while actually ladling out to his readers the most abstruse and difficult religious and political ideas and information. There never was such a master at telling the reader painlessly what he ought to know — and always presented through the minds, the eyes and ears of characters in the story. We know what the Spanish sailors think, what King Philip and Queen Elizabeth do to combat the dangerous epidemic of superstitious fear, even though the Queen herself has a habit of consulting her favorite astrologer, Dr. Dee.

To achieve an easy tone while writing learnedly is granted to the very few — among them, Walter Bagehot. One reads through his book, *The English Constitution,* with continued pleasure. It is only afterward that the reader wonders, How is it possible to write seriously yet wittily about the English constitution? Historians like Mattingly and Bagehot have the habit of reading widely, far beyond the immediate subject. One knows it by their allusions, the flexible analogies and comparisons that inform their pages. Such men have been readers since their youth — what Coleridge liked to call "desultory" readers, who range over the corpus of literature and history without ever losing that delight which old Coke adjured his students to cultivate.

It is something of a marvel that erudition such as Bagehot's or Mattingly's does not spill over and spoil the page. These writers know when to stop and what to leave out. If they are uncertain of the facts they say so, and when they speculate one recognizes at once where fact ends and speculation begins. This brings up the question of historical bias, over which scholars have argued for generations. Has the biographer a right to his personal bias, and how much should he permit it to show?

Of course the biographer is biased! All history is written from a point of view and no one but Almighty God could write with pure objectivity. Carlyle's description of Lord Bacon, quoted on page 82, reveals almost as much of Thomas Carlyle as it does of Bacon; this does not lessen the effect but enhances it. When we read a biography we do not say, Here is a photograph of Florence Nightingale, taken by scientific measurement. We say, Here is what Mrs. Woodham-Smith, who has studied the matter, thinks about Florence Nightingale. In his excellent little book, *The Englishman and His History*, Herbert Butterfield remarks that austerity and objectivity in history cannot derive from the mere personal sincerity and moral rectitude of the individual historian. They need long training, the chastening effects of tradition and criticism.

Picasso has said it more succinctly: "Art is a lie that makes us realize truth." What is at stake is the biographer's historical judgment, which itself has been given many and various names. James Thomson Shotwell (*The History of History*) called it "insight, the first qualification of the historian." Mattingly had a point of view — a bias if you will — concerning the defeat of the Spanish Armada. He looked on the event as transcending national boundaries, an ideological fight, almost a total war, upon the outcome of which hung the fate of all Christendom. When the author conceived his book it was June, 1940, and the Battle of Britain raging — a time, he tells us, "when the eyes of the world were again turned to the shores of England and their surrounding seas."

In writing history or historical biography, the author frequently, perhaps always, has in mind an analogy with today. How else can the historian comprehend but by comparison? Surely, all education and the shaping of intelligence is a matter of learning how to compare, the storing up of enough experience to have points of comparison at hand. Mattingly's analogy, which after all is no more than a suggestion, serves admirably, so that the book holds up a decade later, when the eyes of the world are by no means turned to England.

On the other hand, historical writing can be marred by too direct or persistent an analogy, as witness Carl Van Doren's *The Great Rehearsal*, which treats the Constitutional Convention of 1787 as an introduction to what the author trusts will be the making of a world constitution. Composing his book during the Second World War, it was natural for Van Doren to follow this hopeful lead. Yet we do not read history or biography as prophecy. Or at least we do not so credit it unless the analogy is concealed and the reader permitted to reach his conclusion by himself.

Clarity and seduction in English prose are not easy to achieve: the one stems from clear thinking and knowledge of one's subject; the other is a reflection of the author's personality, his outlook on life, his likes and dislikes, his loves and hates. The balance between historical facts and the biographer's personality, experience, view of life (call it what you will) is an interesting phenomenon to observe upon the printed page. In his *Prometheus*, published when the author was eighty, Maurois tells us, "Balzac set out to be the chronicler of Society; I am simply the chronicler of Balzac." This disarming little statement does not deceive us. The biographer knew well that whatever impression of Balzac's genius he planned to give, history must come into it, the events of Balzac's time as seen by André Maurois.

Historical judgment — the writer's viewpoint on persons and events — also helps with the book's proportion. Scenes in themselves dramatic are not necessarily important to history or to the hero's progress. Yet the temptations are great. For myself I have had an especially hard time with the fascinating murders that cross my biographical path. In Justice Holmes's boyhood the Webster-Parkman murder shook Boston to its foundation. Professor Webster of the Harvard Medical School killed his colleague, Professor Parkman, in a classroom, cut him up with his anatomical saw and hid the remains in various places around the building. During the trial, Dr. Oliver Wendell Holmes, the Justice's father and Professor of Anatomy, was called to the witness stand — which I took as excuse to include the murder. I did so with relish, then shortened the tale bit by bit and ended by putting it in a brief chapter note. After all, young Holmes was eight at the time and to my knowledge never in his life mentioned the incident. Temptation struck again when I found that two delegates to the Constitutional Convention of 1787 were murdered in later life. Judge Lansing of New York went out one evening in Albany to mail a letter down by the wharf and was never seen afterward. The celebrated Chancellor Wythe of Virginia was poisoned by a nephew and heir.

Tailoring, squeezing and jujitsu were needed to fit these murders into *Miracle at Philadelphia* — after which I cut them out again. This time there was not even excuse enough for a footnote.

In sum, *What the reader must know* is a very different proposition from what the writer must know. The biographer must know, as we have said, everything that other biographers have written, plus all he can discover from the records. The reader must know only that which moves the story forward, explains the characters and the scene, and lets him believe what he reads.

11.

*echniques of revealing the hero's thought*

In biographical writing the master can be distinguished from the tyro by the way he lets us know what his characters are thinking. Because he writes history, not fiction, the biographer is never actually "in the hero's mind." Nevertheless his subject is a human being, who feels, grieves, rejoices. A biography that did not give us the hero's thoughts would be a contradiction in terms, besides which it would be irretrievably dull.

The business of telling a subject's thoughts is altogether a technical problem; an author's talent for perception, sympathy, empathy has nothing to do with it. Perhaps a few bad examples will best illustrate the unfortunate effect of, "We can now imagine," or, "It is probable that." An excellent biography of Thomas Jefferson, replete with every scholarly reference, citation, proof, for my taste is ruined by the final page of Volume II. On July 5, 1784, Jefferson sailed for France to take up his duties as minister plenipotentiary. This is a milestone in Jefferson's life, large, important, and we are absorbed in the project — until that final paragraph. It is four o'clock in the morning as the ship puts out to sea:

"What thoughts filled Jefferson's mind as he stood on deck early in the summer morning watching the sun rise over the rugged Boston harbor, is something we can only surmise." Once started, the author goes from bad to worse: "As he turned for a last farewell to that fast receding shore, the sentiments to which he was later to give voice may well have filled his mind. . . ."

Surely — one says — the writer is making this up, even though the quotation that follows is entirely correct, written years later by Jefferson for all the world to read. Perhaps I would not condemn the device so severely had not my own earlier biographies used fictional methods: with Tchaikovsky, the Rubinsteins, Holmes and Adams I transposed letters and diaries into speech and had the characters think or speak accordingly. But with *The Lion and the Throne* (Sir Edward Coke) I turned once and for all to writing biography that contained no fictional devices and documented every quotation.

Over the years, then, I have experimented with various devices to let the reader know what my characters were thinking. Let me say again, this is not a question of the biographer *finding out* the subject's thoughts or emotions, which is a problem of research. Here we are concerned only with how to set down on paper what is in the hero's mind after the writer has discovered, ascertained and checked it with the evidence. In *Beloved Friend* (Tchaikovsky) I first tried out the subjunctive, the *he would* device, which incidentally I afterward discovered in lavish use by academic historians. *Beloved Friend* has a preface — in a burst of fancy I called it a Prelude — the purpose of which was to disarm the musical classicist into sympathy with the whoosh and lilt, the banal and the inspired that is a Tchaikovsky symphony. So personal is this music, so intimate — I wrote — that one feels the composer's actual presence in the concert hall. Is he in the balcony perhaps, hidden characteristically, slipping to the street before anyone can see him?

I finished the scene and took it with the rest of the manuscript to De Voto. "Oh, put all this in the subjunctive," De Voto said. "Always put your own mooning and brooding in the subjunctive." I tried it out and then later found an example in Esther Forbes's *Paul Revere*. Writing of her hero's childhood, with, plainly, little specific evidence; "At first," she says, "the boy's world would be small. His mother's kitchen and the good smells of herbs drying, a suet pudding bubbling on the hearth, ducks roasting. . . . Then there was his father's shop." (The author can now dispense with the subjunctive; she has let us know she is imagining.) "Here was

the smell of charcoal burning in the brick furnace. . . ."
A paragraph of straight description follows, after which
we return to young Revere: "Being social and in no way
self-conscious, the child would enjoy the men and
women who came to the shop."

By now Miss Forbes is moving easily between fact and
speculation. "Hitchbourn Wharf belonged to his grandmother. . . . The North End was a mixture of an almost London elegance of living rubbing shoulders with
poverty and vice." This shifting of tense from condi-
tional to past gives an author latitude to roam in time
and space. Yet the trick (and it is a trick) requires experience; one inch too far and the effect turns silly or
suspect. *Paul Revere* was Miss Forbes's sixth book.

Concerning the *perhaps,* or *it is possible* technique, a
modern biography — an excellent work except for this
recurrent aberration — yields a horrendous display, all
on one page. The book's identity being of no pertinence, I have changed the proper names; italics are
mine. The hero is reading in the university library:

> *Presumably* these extracts were turned over to
> [Professor Smith].
> The extent of [Smith's] contribution to [An-
> son's] effort *we do not, however, know. Perhaps,* it
> is a distortion of reality *to suggest.* . . .
> As [Smith] read the cases in the social law library
> *did he perhaps see* that the practical effort to which
> his working day was dedicated *was not unrelated* to
> the speculative problems to which his evenings
> were given? [Note the ultimate caution — *not un-
> related.*] *We do not know* whether [Smith] as a

theorist accepted or rejected the radical views of Jones. *We do not know* whether as lawyer he sought to provide [Anson] with a political economist's arguments to sustain his lawyer's claim.
All that we can say with confidence is [by this time the reader is too discouraged to care] . . . that there was reciprocating relevance between the day's professional reading and the evening's speculative inquiry.

Later in the book the author tells a superb story about his hero, following which he remarks, "This anecdote, recorded fifty-seven years after the event, may seem so dramatically fitting as to be questionable in its accuracy." As the children say, It isn't fair . . . By such treatment a writer can kill the most brilliant, living material. Better to omit the story altogether.

There are various acceptable ways to take readers into the hero's mind. Even the seemingly fictional *he thought, he felt,* is not fictional if properly handled. It comes best when buttressed before or after with quoted material. In Robert Blake's *Disraeli,* Lady Blessington reads a letter which is quoted on the page. The biographer then continues:

Was he, she wondered, quarrelling about straws? Disraeli replied from Bradenham on January 12 . . . "I really grieve if I said anything which deserved the lecture you gave me."

Or again, the writer can simply tell the subject's feelings.

Disraeli was much mortified at his rebuff. Although he kept the facts of the application and refusal a profound secret, he was bitterly disappointed. As early as February 1842 something of this state of mind appears in a letter to his wife. He feels, he says, "utterly isolated." . . .

Elizabeth Longford in her *Queen Victoria* is adept at this technique.

The Queen no longer tried to admire famous people if she did not like them. The African explorer Stanley she found "a determined ugly little Man — with a strong American twang."

Or again,

Queen Victoria now recognized in herself a certain toughness of character and capacity to handle human situations which her beloved one had lacked. . . . As the years passed, she added to the list of "inevitable" changes which she had accepted philosophically but which the Prince would have opposed . . .

Thomas Carlyle's device of swooping suddenly into the present tense would not be tolerated today. But it is immensely effectual, a brash yet subtle way of entering the subject's mind. Cervantes, shortly before his death, has undertaken a final journey to Madrid:

He has ridden out, I say, to take one other look at the azure firmament and green mosaic pave-

101

ments, and strange carpentry and arras work of this noble Palace of a world.

We are in Cervantes's mind here; it is he (not Carlyle) who sees the arras work of this noble palace, the world. The author has employed not only the present tense but his favorite device of the first-person singular, *I say.* Carlyle had a style wild, brilliant, grotesque, the like of which was never seen before or since. Impossible to imitate him — and undesirable. Yet the biographer, searching for techniques, would do well to range far and wide, not limit himself to his own time and fashions.

A modern biographer who uses the *I think, I believe* device, though sparingly, is Hilda Prescott. In *Mary Tudor,* "I believe" comes seldom; one can count the times. Yet when it comes it does not startle or divert from the business at hand but seems intrinsic, necessary, perfectly natural. On page eighty-four, young Mary, a devout Roman Catholic, signs, under the demand of a brutal father, the articles which deny papal authority and give consent to her father's divorce from her mother, Queen Catherine.

> . . . in a fit of amazed panic [Mary] had been false to her mother and to her mother's Church. She knew what she was doing when she made her surrender. I believe that she never forgot it, and that in every crisis of her life afterwards she remembered it, and in the shadow of that memory, made her decision.

There is a deep thoughtfulness in this which convinces. There is also emotion, the author has not spared herself.

Here is historical imagination, disciplined and sure.
Dame Veronica Wedgwood, an impeccable scholar, has
said that "without passion there might be no errors, but
without passion there would certainly be no history." In
her own celebrated works Miss Wedgwood does not
hesitate a minute to let us know what her people are
thinking.

> The King now dismissed his cares temporarily
> from his mind and went to Newmarket for a hunt-
> ing holiday. . . .
> In this mild season the King became unwillingly
> aware of the disquieting turn that his fortunes had
> so suddenly taken. . . .
> Charles, still unable to believe that anything in
> his government could have provoked such a dem-
> onstration, was sure that his ill-wishers had set the
> people on.

Speaking academically, all of these devices verge on
the fictional. If the thing is well done we believe, we
credit; if ill done we back away, disgusted. A valid but
difficult technique for the author who is about to reveal
a subject's thoughts is an authorial pronouncement of
some universal truth, which in actuality serves to express what one man — the character in question — is
thinking at the moment. This is most feasible in literary
biography, where the hero is apt to be articulate and
witty. Maurois does it beautifully. Observe one brief
scene from *Lélia, The Life of George Sand.* Here
Maurois dissects two characters, entering their minds to
let us know how they felt, what they thought and to

open a door to both natures. I have italicized the key words.

> *Every woman is interested in the men who have been her friends' lovers,* and George examined Didier with an eye that was at once curious and predisposed in his favor. He was good-looking, with somewhat chilly manners — which he owed to his Protestant upbringing — but virile, and much attracted to women. At this, his first meeting with Madame Dudevant [George Sand], he was not impressed. "Rather dry and unforthcoming," he wrote. "She has a remarkable face, but is, I should say, incapable of passion." *The sensual* [Maurois goes on] *have a sure instinct. . . .* Lélia is a woman who denies love. She is beautiful, she is fine, but she is cold as a statue. "How shall I free myself from this marble envelope," she says, "which . . . holds me as totally imprisoned as a corpse by its tomb."

Perhaps the skill of this is not at first apparent. Maurois is helped by having a heroine who wrote an autobiographical novel, infinitely revealing and often quoted — a convenience of which no doubt Maurois was aware when he chose George Sand as subject. Not every writer, however, achieves the worldly wisdom which enables him to open his paragraphs with Maurois's likely observations on life and love. Age ripens and the old master's hand is quick. He plays with his phrases as so many bright balls tossed in air, yet never a word too many, nothing for show. All pertains; the pattern is not broken.

12.

 *eparate scenes. Court trials. The flashback. Historical chestnuts*

To plot scenes as they come due is for the writer almost like plotting a new biography each time. First there is the added research; a folder of notes that had been slim becomes three folders or four. A careful chronology must be made, moving hour by hour down the day or days of climax. Each new scene moreover presents a decision as to *means of perception,* as they call it in creative-writing classes. I have never liked the phrase. With me the problem takes other terms, such as the shift from being in scene to being out of scene. Is the writer in the hero's mind or in the public mind? Suppose one is describing a state wedding in a cathedral. Evidence permitting, it can be done through the eyes of the bride's mother in the front row — from inside the scene. It can be told from reported rumors among the crowd waiting outside or through news sheets next day — the public mind.

Stringent exercise in this technique came to me in the course of writing about criminal trials in court. Coke's biography had five. I found them difficult to handle; perhaps my own experience, flounderings, backings and fillings will be the clearest explanation of something that defies brief definition. The first three trials were for treason, in Coke's day a capital crime, carrying the fearful penalty of torture and death on the scaffold. A state trial was less an arraignment in today's sense than a grand spectacle arranged by the crown — the state — as example to the nation. Guilt was foreordained, predetermined. Permitted no counsel, the prisoner relied entirely upon his own eloquence in defense. He stood in the box facing a vast assembly and conducted a day-long sparring match with the Attorney General and the judges. To inform of these procedures was an intrinsic part of Coke's biography.

The Earl of Essex was first, then Sir Walter Ralegh and then the Gunpowder conspirators of 1605. Each trial presented the same initial difficulty: where to begin. Should the story open in court, with the witnesses giving testimony and thus themselves telling the story of their treason? Or should one open with the actual crime, describe the plotters and proceed incident by incident, so that when the prisoner stood in the box and witnesses were interrogated the reader needed no reference to past events, which always slow up a story. The evidence was extensive, from Cobbett's *State Trials* to accounts written by contemporary historians such as William Camden, or the letters of spectators. King James himself could be described, crouched at the listening hole or behind an arras. The problem, in short, was one of presentation; if the scenes failed it would be nobody's fault but the biographer's.

Anyone who today attends a criminal trial knows before he enters court just what the crime was, when it allegedly took place and so on. *What the reader must know* is therefore, in trial scenes, vital to the narrative process. Here the biographer can learn much from the playwright. In John Marquand's book, *Thirty Years,* he says, "a very competent playwright once told me that after one minute and a half, at the longest, the audience must know enough about the main characters to be interested in them and enough about the general direction which the play will take, to wish to follow further. In this respect there is one thing that must never be forgotten. There is no conceivable excuse for boredom, on artistic grounds, or on any others whatsoever."

This terrifying precept called for experiment, the trying out of every method. I sorted the evidence and wrote my first trial scene both ways, in full — opening in court and then starting again with the enactment of the crime. The double procedure was laborious but it paid off; the evidence was thereby laid out before me end to end on the page, away from the distracting mass of file cards.

Lord Essex was Queen Elizabeth's handsome favorite. Thirty-four years old at his trial, he faced Edward Coke as prosecutor, also eight judges and a jury of twenty-five peers of the realm. An appalling amount of preliminary information was needed before the reader could understand, not only trial procedure (so different from today), but also the Elizabethan politics, the personal ambition and vanity which lay at the heart of this young lord's defection, and upon which all court testimony was to be based. I began therefore very early in the story. "Rebellion," I wrote, "does not come by sudden chance. The hen must sit before the egg is hatched, the citadel does not fall until it is weakened from within — and the greatest lord of England, unless he has a history behind him, does not run through London with two hundred swordsmen, crying out to the citizens that he is betrayed."

This of course was a fairly obvious device. But again, when one has a story to tell one cannot be choosy, one must simply take the dive. My beginning carried us back in time. "Long before that fatal February Sunday [so runs the next paragraph] trouble was indicated. Essex's jealousy had become proverbial. . . ." The word *proverbial* puts us in London's mind, England's mind, and gives leeway to cast back some years to Essex's reprehensible behavior as a general of the armies in Ireland. Every trial scene, whether fiction or history, makes use of the flashback, a device vitally necessary to biographers, and so familiar that it needs no further definition. One thing, however, the writer learns: short flashbacks can deal only in fact. Asides, author speculation, shift of grammatical tense, all are fatal; the movement must be rapid and the tone maintained or confusion ensues. Confusion means loss of credibility. And once a reader ceases to believe, he is gone, the story is forfeit. Fact can be harder to credit than fiction; the biographer must stay strictly within limits, permit himself no offstage roaming.

Lord Essex's trial was held in the legendary vastness of Westminster Hall, which fortunately needed no more than a word of description, having already been described in another connection. I wrote the scene from inside. The reader is present, among the audience. "Essex was dressed in black from head to foot. Those sitting near noted that his face was troubled at first, 'somewhat unsettled,' but that it soon cleared and he stood at ease. . . . As the Clerk's voice droned on, describing the tumult at Essex House, the crazy run through the city, Essex showed open contempt — 'smiled several times and lifted up his eyes to Heaven.' "

The quotations came from contemporary accounts, both official and private. In the end the roll is called and the jury of peers announces its verdict. The Lord Steward receives the white wand of office, holds it above his head and in the ancient symbolic gesture, breaks it in two. Lord Essex's fate is sealed. The end of a court trial is no problem. It tells itself, though there is always more to add — in this case the commutation of torture and hanging because of the prisoner's noble birth. Also the fact that after an ignoble confession which implicated his friends and even his sister, Essex was beheaded on Tower Hill.

So far so good. But what of the ensuing trials, equally important to Coke's career? Sir Walter Ralegh was the next victim and Coke's brutality to that gallant knight as he stood in the prisoner's box was to become legendary. Legendary also — and equally true historically — were the eloquence and poetry of Ralegh's self-defense. When the day of trial began Sir Walter, as we have said, was the most unpopular man in England. When it ended and the news had time to spread, a witness wrote that "never was man so hated and so popular in so short a time."

How was the biographer to treat this? Obviously with truth according to the records, and no sparing of Edward Coke. Yet judgment must not be passed upon the Attorney General as if this trial had been held today, with today's rules of evidence and today's tradition that a man is innocent until proven guilty. What Attorney General Coke did and said accorded with the rules of the time, which in the modern opinion would be no rules at all; from start to finish the thing was rigged in favor of the crown.

I have heard academic historians condemn a colleague for letting "presentism" inform his pages. The word is not in the dictionary, but I take it the professors meant writing of the past in terms of today. This indeed could be a pitfall. But a greater one was the danger that Sir Walter Ralegh would run away with the book. Elizabeth's great sea-fighter, explorer, poet, defender of the realm, on trial for treason? Nothing could be more paradoxical and more dramatic; as a scene it could upstage the burning of Rome. If it were written from inside, if readers were permitted to be present in the audience (and the evidence warranted it), then indeed Coke's biography might change heroes in midstream.

But if the tale of that day's work were merely told in my own words, I could be on safer ground. And for this purpose, the shorter the narrative, the better.

In the end I threw away all caution and wrote the scene from inside at full length, with all of Coke's brutality and Ralegh's gallantry exposed face to face. There are times — we have said it before — when a biographer must forget the "scheme," forget his self-made rules and jump in, swimming boldly with the material. This is what history tells us truly happened. And this, at whatever risk, is what we must tell. Opposite the title page of his life of Tolstoi, Ernest Simmons printed some words from his hero.

> I clearly realize that my biography, if it suppressed all the nastiness and criminality of my life — as they customarily write biographies — would be a lie, and that if one is going to write my biography, one must write the whole truth.

Whether he aims at hagiology or debunking, the biographer would do well to keep these words in mind. Moreover the very length of a scene can make a hazard, as with Ralegh's trial. Two and a half chapters out of the book's thirty-five seemed a trifle disproportionate, and when Ralegh came to his arraignment, Edward Coke was barely past fifty and had thirty-three active years ahead. Concerning separate scenes in a biography, length is indeed something to consider. Written too concisely a scene can be lifeless, a mere listing of facts and events, with no movement in it and little color. Teachers of composition I think make too much of brevity. Too-short can kill as surely as too-long, and a great scene should not be composed like a telegram, especially at the first writing. That master storyteller, Rudyard Kipling, in his memoirs testifies that when, to save trouble, he wrote short *ab initio,* "much salt went out of the work."

There is also to be considered how the biographer's big scenes fit with previous and following chapters. If Coke's five court trials had followed each other *en suite* the reader could not have stomached it; such fare is too rich for digestion. After Ralegh's arraignment came the trial of the eight young gentlemen who planned to blow up the Parliament House and King James and the legislators with it — the Gunpowder Plot of 1605. Fortunately, two years intervened and one could concentrate on something pleasanter. Thirteen years later came the trial of Lord and Lady Somerset for poisoning a courtier, Sir Thomas Overbury. Lastly, in the year 1621, Lord Bacon's impeachment by Parliament.

Obviously the reader would not accept complete participation in five courtroom scenes. The last three therefore must be quicker paced, told more or less from the public viewpoint, outside the courtroom. In short, the reader could be at one time inside and outside the scene — made possible by intense public interest in the events and much evidence thereto. The Somerset trials were managed in five pages, Bacon's impeachment in eleven, as opposed to forty-two for Ralegh. Much could now be done by hint and suggestion, the reader being already familiar with seventeenth-century courtroom procedure. No explanation was needed when a judge stepped from the bench to testify, or when the fearful penalty of disembowelment, hanging and quartering was pronounced. Every court trial for capital offense is by its nature exciting. It was to be hoped therefore that readers, happily enmeshed, had swallowed the large doses of legal history as earlier administered; doses intrinsic to the plot and plan. On the wall was the shadow of the noose, the axe; one trusted it would hold the reader until the end.

If this account of five court trials is itself lengthy, let it serve as a warning! Even so it is pertinent here to mention the biographer's awful and continued wrestling with the facts themselves as given in the sources. These, as every historian knows, have a way of backing off at the last moment or turning inside out, disproving themselves, placing the hero in Norfolk when at that date he should rightly have been in London, or marrying him at twenty when the Lady B ——'s letter to her mother plainly fixes it at twenty-one.

Sometimes the fault is the biographer's; a date, an erroneous fact sets itself in the mind and stays there, to the subsequent ruin of a scene. Ralegh's trial, for instance, was held at Winchester, "in the Castle," the records said. I went to Winchester and climbed the hill to the Royal Castle, a weathered stone pile which dominates the town. In the Great Hall, where court trials still are held, I filled a notebook with description, the hush and echo of voices under an arched roof, Arthur's round table at the western end above the royal dais and the famed pillar rubbed shiny by the backs of talking lawyers who had leaned against it during the centuries. But by the time I was ready to write the scene, some years later, I discovered that Ralegh's trial was not held in "the Castle" at all, but down the hill in Wolvesey Castle, the old episcopal palace of which nothing remains. Apparently no one in Winchester had been aware of it, the word Wolvesey had slipped by me in the records and I fell upon my error only by chance.

As always in these cases, despair took over. Such lapses can destroy a biographer for days, until that proverbial moment when he summons resolution to throw out his scene entire and begin anew, whereupon he finds that much can be salvaged. After all, Ralegh was imprisoned beneath the Great Hall. His cell looked out on the green Hampshire Valley below; from behind bars he could hear the sentinel's horn blow for the city gates to open, a voice like a wild beast's call — and there was no reason the biographer should not make the most of it.

Writing these trials brought up also the problem of historical chestnuts. The Gunpowder Plot is a chestnut: *"Remember remember the Fifth of November, Gunpowder treason and plot."* One hesitates to undertake such a tired tale. The only recourse is to forget all one has heard and go back to original documents. Immediately — as in describing George Washington — the thing comes to life. Who would have thought that the tallest of the eight conspirators, tunneling under the Parliament House, would have suffered from cramps in the legs? One forgets that fine gentlemen are amateurs with pick and shovel. And how surprising to find the plotters at their night work, refreshing themselves with "baked meats, hard eggs and pasties." (Sandwiches! But no, the

Fourth Earl of Sandwich was not yet born.) The biographer is caught up, he is on his way.

There are writers — one reads of them in the book reviews — who never rewrite, whose first version stands clear and gemlike before the world. To these, if truly they exist, this book has nothing to say. It is addressed to another species altogether: writers who mold their stories by trial and error, chip at them as the sculptor with his marble. To these it cannot be said too often: Get your story down on paper. Cover the pages, right or wrong. Never mind how scared you are and how exposed you feel. Have something on hand that can be worked with, shaped, framed to a finish. Kipling recommends, after the first one or two revisions, reading the work aloud, "alone and at leisure. Maybe a shade more brushwork will then indicate or impose itself. If not, praise Allah and let it go, and 'when thou hast done, repent not.' "

Reading aloud alone is surely part of composition. Reading aloud to a listener can be an even more taxing exercise; when interest flags, listeners fidget. Moreover, a badly constructed sentence bumps and stumbles notably when heard. Reading to listeners carries however so much danger that one dares not recommend it. Too many authors read aloud simply to hear their works praised. Edward Gibbon's *Autobiography* disposes of the whole idea in short order: "I was soon disgusted with the modest practice of reading the manuscript [*The Decline and Fall*] to my friends. Of such friends some will praise from politeness, and some will criticize from vanity."

13.

 *uoted material. Translations, cita-*
tions, footnotes. When we do
not know

Biography by its nature includes much quoted material, which can become tedious unless dexterously handled. Success here is an absolute necessity of the craft. In reading aloud one should not have to add those ugly words, "quote unquote"; the paragraph should flow plainly and explicitly from cited phrases to the author's comment. One method is to begin with indirect quotation: It was his opinion . . . she had always believed . . .

then use a direct quotation as climax. In short: choose a telling phrase from a letter, diary, speech — perhaps five words, perhaps five sentences. Lead up to it by indirect quotation which prepares the reader, then loose the bright shaft at the end.

Mattingly does this often in *The Armada,* moving easily from indirect to direct speech:

> . . . the Amsterdam printers expatiated on the natural catastrophes in store for everybody. There would be violent tempests, they promised, and terrible floods . . .
>
> Very few English almanacs survive for 1588 . . . Walter Gray's may be taken as typical. In the general prediction for winter he says, "Here . . . might be noted, according to artificial skill, many strange events to happen . . . God . . . turn all evils away from us. Amen. . . . There is likelihood of an earthquake with fear of the plague and pestilence."

The effect is achieved by various methods; writers can try them out. Observe Mattingly again, at a moment of casting back over the years. Here we have a change of time and tense — *who once had written . . . now wrote . . . now had to hear.* We have the author's own viewpoint — king and sea dog exchanging characters — and we have again the weaving in and out between direct and indirect quotation:

> Indeed, in the strange correspondence of that winter the prudent king and the daring sea dog

seemed to have exchanged characters. The king who once had written, "In so great an enterprise as that of England, it is fitting to move with feet of lead," now wrote, "Success depends mostly upon speed. Be quick!" and the captain who had once argued for a bold blow at the main enemy and against the folly of delay and defensive war now had to hear his own arguments turned against him, while he mumbled about the imprudence of leaving the Spanish coasts undefended, and the unwisdom of undertaking a campaign not thoroughly prepared.

Once mastered, such a technique can be one of the sharpest tools of the biographer's trade. There is, further, the seemingly simple matter of how to introduce a direct quotation. If this is done clumsily the entire illusion can be destroyed. The 1920's saw a revolt against fancy ways of announcing that he said or she said. The edict went out against *He shouted . . . "No!" he stormed . . . "Oh, please do," she pouted.* For quick dramatic exchange, there is no doubt that plain *he said, she said* are effectual, as is the device of omitting all verbs meaning *to speak.* This last however results in a stark succession of quoted sentences following each other down the page, and can be confusing. Readers may have to count back to see who is talking.

It is the fiction writers who usually set new styles. Yet there is no reason for biographers to be bound by any literary fashion, new or old. David Cecil in *The Young Melbourne* ignores the new mode and uses — very effectively — a number of verbs for *said* and *spoke,* with qualifying adverbs more often than not. (None of the quoted material that follows is fictional, all of it comes unchanged from source material.)

"Don't let Edward Bulwer let you down," she adjured her ominously. . . .

"Shall we meet," he would be heard murmuring to himself, "shall we meet in another world?" . . .

"Go and be damned," he had retorted. . . .

David Cecil is a virtuoso in this technique. His every qualifying word helps the characterization and moves the paragraph along, occasionally establishing time and place. " 'Hart and C.,' writes Lady Bessborough from Lismore Castle, where they were staying with her uncle Hartington, 'had many disputes on the damp.' " The interpolated clause, a trifle long and clumsy, is redeemed by the fact that it fixes the reader in time and situation. Too many biographies leap from place to place or year to year, to the mystification of the reader. Better to come right out with dates on the page; readers hate hunting back to discover if we are still in the year 1750 — or is it already 1751?

Cecil's qualifying words in these cases are felicitous, which is perhaps why we accept them; they point up the quotation. " 'When they say this to me,' remarked the exasperated Lady Bessborough, 'I want to bellow.' " And speaking of Melbourne's furiously emotional wife, " 'The storm outside,' said William to her with rueful humour, 'is hardly more than that inside.' " Quoted speech belonging to remote centuries needs qualification or explanation where the idiom is hard to understand; the ancient customs are by now forgotten. Miss Jenkins in *Elizabeth the Great* is skillful with this.

> [Lord Bacon] wanted a bathing-pool with sides and bottom "embellished with coloured glass and such things of lustre," but the fashionable enlargement of windows in the facade of great houses which caused the saying: "Hardwick Hall, more glass than wall," seemed to him at the end of the century, to have been overdone. He said: "You shall have sometimes fair houses so full of glass, that one cannot tell where to become to be out of the sun or cold."

A good place to note indirect conversation is the *New Yorker* magazine, where writers manipulate it in every conceivable version. Concerning the idiomatic quotation which must be preceded by explanation, the playwrights, Lindsay and Crouse, once told me, "When we write a gag and the audience doesn't laugh, it's never the gag that's at fault, it's the lead-up." For the biographer this can be true whether he aims for a laugh or a tear. When the quotation appears the reader must be ready for it.

Biography needs care also in the use of old, familiar quotations; to announce these as if they were new is unfortunate. "I can't tell a lie," said George; "I did cut it with my hatchet." The reader is bored unless the writer takes him into his confidence, reminding rather than informing. "All the world remembers . . ." or,

"As every schoolboy is aware . . ." Note Robert Blake's clever technique in *Disraeli*, where his hero "ate half the pie and drank all the champagne, and it was then he paid his famous compliment [to Mary Ann]: 'Why my dear, you are more like a mistress than a wife.' "

A question I am frequently asked is, "How do you translate foreign quotations — right there on the page, or below in a footnote?" Of course one need not translate at all, there is no rule. One can leave whole paragraphs in the original Latin, staring up as a challenge. British scholars assume that anybody who can read, can read Greek; they seldom bother to translate. Baffled and infuriated by this, I long ago resolved to translate from even the most familiar foreign tongue, and as tactfully as possible so the reader would not feel he was being patronized. Nobody wants to be addressed (for example) *de haut en bas* — looked down upon. In the English version of *Lélia,* Maurois prints in French a witty verse of de Musset's, then translates it in a footnote.* The eye follows obediently downward because we know from experience that something amusing will be found.

* "Oh, Monsieur Latouche, sleep sound."

The matter of footnotes and chapter notes can be of utmost importance to biographers, beyond the mere convention of giving sources for quoted material or citing authorities for statements of fact that need bolstering. In *Mary Tudor,* Miss Prescott arranges her notes by chapters — hundreds of notes which give nothing but straight information as to where historical evidence can be found. Occasionally however she cites opposing evidence, then gives her decision: "I therefore suppose that the episode took place on the day [Northumberland] arrived at Cambridge." Miss Prescott lets nothing slip by without its reference.

When a citizen of London spent the evening out, supping with friends at Henley on Thames, the vast meal, enlivened by "12 wassails, and maidens singing with them," concluded with dishes of spices and fruit "as marmalade, ginger bread, jelly, comfits, sugar plate."[58]

Here chapter note 58 hardly seems necessary, as the next sentence tells us how "that same worthy citizen, Henry Machyn, the undertaker, recorded another feast in his diary." Perhaps Miss Prescott, though known as a thoroughly reliable scholar, was extra meticulous because her previous book had been a novel — that glorious, somber tale set in the time of Henry VIII, *The Man on a Donkey*.

Every graduate student knows something of the techniques of citation. Yet there is great difference in how authors handle such matters, and the differences are worth noting. Historians can suffer serious pangs over the possibility that something they wrote may have been unconsciously taken from another author. Observe the following almost distracted sentence from Catherine Strateman's edition of *The Liverpool Tractate*, a valuable and learned book: "To avoid the charge of plagiarism it may be proper to mention that the substance of the latter part of this chapter is taken in a manner wholly from Scobell and this I believe is the only place where I have made use of any author without quoting his name which I should have done here but that I have both added to and retrenched from him and likewise inverted the order of his narration."

David Cecil has his references at the back, but we do not need them. His "List of Authorities" is like no other on earth — offhand, dégagé, and supremely confident. Lord Cecil wears his learning lightly. To demand further proof would be like asking Charles Lamb to annotate the essay on roast pig.

Mattingly has no footnotes in *The Armada*. But his "General Note on Sources" is masterly, divided into "Archives and Manuscript Collections; Published Sources; Contemporary Narrative; Modern Authorities." The chapter notes are interesting enough to read straight through, disregarding specific references. We recognize them as asides, unsuitable for the text, where they would retard the story, but pertinent and pleasant reading. The following belongs to Chapter XXII of *The Armada*. One's eye skips over the hieroglyphics, though reassured by them:

> Several Italian ambassadors got copies of a sketch for a "crescent" formation for the Armada (Flor. *Arch. Med.*, 4919, fol. 340); Novara to Montalto, 4 June 1588 (Vat. *Spagna*, 38); Canciano to the duke (Arch. di Stato, Mantova, Esterni, 601). One of these must have formed the basis of Filippo Pigafetta, *Discorso sopra l'ordi-*

nanza dell'armata catolica (Rome, 1588), see Corbett, II, 220ff. Pigafetta's rather pedantic description is more elaborate and impractical than the sketches, but it is clear from the Spanish narratives, as well as from English references, that the Armada did normally proceed in a sort of crescent formation, not unlike that shown in Adams's charts, but with the horns projecting much farther to the rear.

Occasionally we wonder why such material is indeed not part of the text. Stephen Birmingham in *Our Crowd, The Great Jewish Families of New York,* is wildly lavish with footnotes. A few are straight reference:

> * *Our Times, Pre-War America,* by Mark Sullivan (Scribners).

Some give bits of information:

> * In addition to his nephew, he had the Neustadts, who were parents-in-law of his son Morti.

Some tell of events that occurred after the time span of the text:

> * As a result, in Jewish circles in New York today one can always speculate whether so-and-so, with his German name, is really a German or a secret Pole or Russian.

Many of Birmingham's footnotes are highly amusing. On page 286 the text informs us that Felix Warburg had always wanted a herd of cows. "So they acquired one."*

> * And with it a herdsman as flamboyant as Felix, who immediately ordered stationery printed which said, at the top in large letters, "WOODLANDS FARM, WILLIAM B. JONES, SUPERINTENDENT," and, at the bottom, in very small letters, "Felix M. Warburg, owner."

Our Crowd is an immensely popular book, written in a racy style, more like a series of articles in a Sunday-newspaper magazine. It is also brilliantly perceptive and consistently entertaining. However, a writer like Cecil or Mattingly would never have been satisfied with this manner of dropping footnotes which to all appearances were troublesome to incorporate in the text. The effect is that of a man making a speech and turning aside occasionally for a joke or a justification of his subject matter.

An author can be helped by his footnotes — and he can be driven to the wall by them. Edmund C. Burnett edited, in eight stout volumes, the *Letters of Members of the Continental Congress*. After this work of enormous erudition, which teems with footnotes and is in constant use by scholars today, Burnett wrote a volume called *The Continental Congress*. By this time the author was sick of annotation and states as much in a tone exasperated and refreshing: "Inevitably," says his preface, "some addict to modern historiography, if perchance any such should venture in amongst these pages, will inquire, Why no footnotes? To which the author will be tempted to blurt out the reply, why should there be? Is it not reasonable to indulge the hope that any student of the Revolution will be able to find his way through the narrative without feeling the impulsion to pause and consult some source or other? For such, however, as require the stimulating cocktail of footnotes or bibliography, let this suffice: the basic source of the narrative is the *Letters of Members* previously mentioned."

It requires a splendidly self-confident author thus to scold his readers; perhaps it could not be done outside the academic world. The guild of historians knows how to laugh at itself as well as how to tear a member's hide off; it would seem that both exercises are salutary. There exist however so many styles and formats for citation that a biographer sometimes hesitates at the threshold. In preparing a bibliography for *The Lion and the Throne* I was puzzled what to include. Should it be only the original sources, printed as well as manuscript? Or should I name the many books, whether primary or tertiary, that gave me scenes and characterization? The sly paperback called *Our Old Nobility* might go in, and so on through the famous Parliamentary diarists, down to the gossip writers of Coke's time — delightful and scurrilous reporters whom old Isaac Disraeli called *"les on dit,"* who gave us the *"pourquoi of the pourquoi."* A professor of history, eminent in her field, urged me to put in everything, even the King James Bible, which after all was translated during Coke's middle years. The professor said she wanted a bibliography that would show how a biographer went about composing, so that students could follow through and see where the scenes or characters came from, chapter to chapter.

Studying the scholarly methods of one's colleagues and noting degrees of conscientiousness (or anxiety) displayed by the more luxuriant footnoters, the biographer realizes once again that facts alone will not tell his story. Facts can, indeed, lead him astray unless he is at all times aware of *proportion* — let alone charm — in his presentation. George Canning* once remarked that "nothing is so fallacious as facts, except figures." As the writer progresses it dawns on him, perhaps in his third book, that there are things the reader *need not know,* need never be told. Does it matter, for instance, who George Canning was, above? The fact that he is quoted shows he was important, and the curious reader can look him up. It is not necessary, in one's story, to resolve every riddle. For example, was Ralegh guilty of treason? Everything in us cries out, No! Yet if innocent, why did he early inform us against his friend, Lord Cobham, and why does his testimony in court contradict itself? Or take the question of Lord Bacon's moral guilt in the impeachment of 1620. Parliament proved Lord Bacon to be guilty. But, everybody in Elizabeth's parsimonious government lived on bribes, though these enjoyed the name of perquisites, New Year's gifts, gratuities, grants. Even the renowned statesman, Robert Cecil, enjoyed a pension from the Spanish enemy in return for certain favors. Surely the writer had best present the evidence on both sides and leave moral judgment to the reader?

* English statesman, 1770–1827. (Awkward footnote, and typical. Why not, rather, in the text, "A prime minister of England, George Canning . . .")

A convenient technique for biographers is the use of a white space to indicate a time lapse, like a curtain or scrim in the theater while the scene is changed. "Turn back, then, to the year 1579." Elizabeth Longford does this often in *Queen Victoria:*

> The Queen said good-bye with regret to an old year, "which seemed to have become an old friend" and whose successor might well not be so friendly.
>
> [*White Space*]
>
> "The year opens gloomily," the Queen wrote on 1 January 1854.

The device works equally for a change of pace or scene, or a shift in the means of perception. In the example below, Longford moves from being directly in the scene to being in the public mind:

> . . . Lady Flora had died a little after two; "the poor thing died without a struggle & only just raised her hands & gave one gasp . . ."
>
> [*White Space*]
>
> The result of this tragic death was another flare-up of public scandal. The post-mortem, which Lady Flora had desired . . .

It would be possible to go on indefinitely, discussing convenient techniques. One question, however, seems to come oftener than any other. "What happens when you run into, say, a ten-year interval and nothing to put in it?" One way out of this is to skip the interval boldly either by a new chapter, a white space or a brief statement to the effect that the records do not reveal . . . the records are nonexistent . . . were destroyed . . . or simply, "We do not know." When Conyers Read was writing his life of William Cecil, Lord Burghley, I told him I was eager to learn about a certain period of Burghley's life that hitherto had been unexplained. I couldn't wait, I said, to hear what happened. "Well, you *won't* hear what happened," Read replied gloomily. "Because we don't know anything about those ten years. And a lifetime of search wouldn't yield the information."

I asked what he proposed to do, then, and the professor retorted, "What are *you* doing with Edward Coke between 1571 and 1581, before he began reporting his law cases?" (Actually, Read said "between '71 and '81." Scholars who are at home in their period seldom designate the century in conversation. They are like Bostonians who refer to "the Magazine" or "the President" when they mean the *Atlantic Monthly* or the head of Harvard.)

Authors in earlier times had an advantage in this matter of meeting a blank passage of time. Somewhere in those twenty-four volumes called *Old Parliamentary History** — delicious and invaluable source for the debates of Lords and Commons up to 1660 — the author

* *The Parliamentary or Constitutional History of England* . . . (1066–1660). London, 1751–1761. Vol. IV, p. 342. Readers can judge if this footnote helps the text.

suddenly breaks out as follows: "We have now a gap of time, of near four years, and nothing material to fill it up with."

Such frank confession makes things easier for the historian. Thomas Fuller published, in 1662, an immensely helpful work in three volumes, entitled *Worthies of England* — a gossipy, reliable source for biographers, divided into counties and subdivided under the headings of Sheriffs, Prelates, Gentry, Statesmen, and so on. When he comes to Yorkshire, Fuller bounds along until he reaches his heading of *Statesmen,* when he stops short. "Pardon, reader," he says, "my postponing this topic of statesmen, being necessitated to stay a while for further information."

How pleasing it would be if we were permitted such asides today! I for one enjoy the direct address to the reader; we lost a valuable crutch when we discarded that particular literary technique.

Perhaps none of the questions asked in these "technical" chapters can be answered with complete satisfaction. One cannot make rules. The writer tries out different methods; he experiments, discovers what is right for *him.* I knew a woman, somewhat tone-deaf, whose ambition was to sing alto in a small chorus. She taught herself to sing intervals by chanting a major fifth whenever she drove her car around a righthand turn, a minor sixth when she rounded to the left, and so on through the harmonic scale.

In all the arts, surely there is no technique that does not improve with practice, given the heart to persist.

14.

refaces

There is a tradition in the publishing business that readers usually skip prefaces. This seems to me unfortunate, besides being an act almost incomprehensible. Surely, the reader wants to know why a book has been written, especially if it is history or biography, and wishes to know also the biographer's credentials for undertaking the work. Is the author an authority on this particular subject; has he written upon it before; where did he find his material; is he just returned from Outer Mongolia or did he come upon all this in the New York Public Library?

A preface can serve something of the same purpose as the introduction of a speaker on the public stage, which if properly handled helps both audience and performer. On the platform a too long introduction is a bore but a too short one can be disconcerting; a speaker does not want to stand up and be thrown unannounced to the wolves. Audience or book readers: these are the enemy and must be cajoled or conquered.

A good writer is desperately serious about his preface. In a three-year book he has probably written the foreword three or four times a year at least; these pages tell what his book is about. And to know confidently and specifically what his book is about can be, as already designated, the most pertinent problem a biographer faces. Among modern prefaces Miss Jenkins's is beautifully explicit. "The aim of this book," she says, "was to collect interesting personal information about Queen Elizabeth I. . . . There is nothing in the book which has not already been published in some form but some of it is, I believe, very little known; historians have not room in their books for such matters and the popular writers have not made use of them."

This seems to me a very necessary statement, answering the question, "What can there be new about Queen Elizabeth; what has the author discovered that we did not know?" Yet Miss Jenkins is neither apologetic nor defiant; simply, she tells what she has set out to do, and conversely — but only by implication — what she has not set out to do. It is a temptation to fill up a preface by

anxious statements of what the book is *not* about; this
stems largely from the author's sense of responsibility as
a historian; it is a continuation of arguments he has had
with himself during the years of composition. While
writing *John Adams and the American Revolution* I
was much troubled because there was no room for more
than a mention of the West Indies trade, so important
to New England, or of British internal politics under
George III, and whether Canada should be given up in
favor of Guadaloupe; or even of the problem of Indians
at home. Yet all were vital questions of the day, and
though I could not see that Adams had anything to do
with placating, fighting or generally disposing of the Six
Nations, the Continental Congress was forever wrestling
with the subject.

I must have written four full prefaces beginning,
"This is not a book about . . ." In the end I included
no word of it. An author who does use such an opening,
and cleverly, is Stephen Birmingham in his preface to
Our Crowd. "It was my intention," he says, "when I
undertook this book, *not* to write a book that would be
simply 'about rich people.' " The book of course *is*
about rich people, it cannot help but be. The author's
seeming deprecation is less apology for himself than for
the stupendous affluence of his characters in an era
newly poverty-conscious.

Actually it is at times imperative to tell the reader
what a book does not purport to be. In such case the
shorter the statement the better. "This is a life of
Balzac. A life, not a critical study." Thus the old master,
Maurois, opening his Author's Foreward to *Prometheus.*
At once, we know that we are not launched on a flight

into the higher criticism; a man will live and breathe in these pages, the author's reputation gives promise to his statement.

In a biography about a little-known subject it is logical to have a preface telling why the subject seems important enough for a book. Importance can stem from nothing more than love, as in *Grandmother Brown's Hundred Years.* Anybody who is loved is important, providing the author has skill to convince us. Perhaps a person, vastly significant to his era, has been forgotten and must be revived. Or perhaps the political temper of one's own time inspires or drives a writer to recall other times and braver men. *The Lion and the Throne* was written during the Joseph McCarthy era. Through Edward Coke's stubborn defiance of a Stuart king I hoped to show the origin of our civil liberties under a free constitutional government. The preface told why a book about an almost unknown Englishman pertained to life in the United States today.

On the other side of the picture, some explanation is needed for presenting still another biography of a very famous person, as with Miss Jenkins, whose book, as I have said, aimed for a special, very personal view of her heroine. Reappraisal of a historical character can however be undertaken for a number of reasons. The rapid advance of science has invalidated old ideas, or perhaps a new scientific theory calls for a background of history to explain its development. To the dedicated scholar it is of course incredible that the world knows nothing of his hero, this man who lived long ago but who to the writer is more familiar than his neighbors on Elm

Street. "Considering the significance of the subject it is surprising that no adequate life of William Cecil, Lord Burghley, has ever been written." To most people this may not be surprising in the least. Yet the historian's passion, his indignation are appealing. If Professor Read feels so deeply, then this Burghley must be worth knowing about.

It is good when the author's emotion comes through. Dr. Oliver Wendell Holmes, the Justice's father, as a young physician of thirty-four published a daring essay on "The Contagiousness of Puerperal Fever" — this in a day when the profession looked on such an idea as nonsense and, in so untried a practitioner, supremely impudent. "I am too much in earnest for either humility or vanity," wrote Holmes, "but I do entreat those who hold the keys of life and death to listen to me also for this once." A hundred and twenty-five years later the reader again is stirred. Courage, like truth, "is a great word, and one that makes the heart beat."

The writer of a preface is beset by various temptations. One is the urge to recount his whole story then and there, as if to say, "Look what I have to tell! Is not this marvelous?" The modern book jacket, however, performs its service well enough; the writer can save his words. Another temptation is to confess one's troubles in a preface, let the world know what the author has suffered during composition these three years or twenty. In a less sophisticated age this was not only permissible but could be charming. Says Anthony à Wood, in the foreword to his celebrated *History of Oxford University,* "A painful work it is I'll assure you, and more than difficult, wherein what toyle hath been taken, as no man thinketh so no man believeth, but he that hath made the tryall."

What biographer but longs to say this to his readers! Surely, the public should be made to appreciate what he has gone through? Or again, from another century, "beseeching you that where you shall find any faults, which by my insufficiency, the intricateness of the worke, or the printer's recklessness are committed, either friendly to pardon, or by some means to admonish me thereof."

Friendly to pardon: the writer's hopes are vain. Once the book is published, his every mistake will echo hollowly back to him. Yet there is no reason a preface should not entice the reader, endeavor to draw him in. Every merchant sets out his wares as attractively as possible; a preface should not bore the reader or shut the door in his face. Authors in earlier centuries were well aware of this; now and again a preface even ventures to share the joys of composition, as Izaak Walton's *The Compleat Angler.* "I wish the reader to take notice," says his foreword, "that in the writing of it I have made myself a recreation of a recreation; and that it might prove so to him, and not read dull, and tediously, I have in severall places mixt . . . some innocent harmless mirth."

How altogether disarming, especially as Walton's text lives up to his promise! In our own time, Sheila Kaye-Smith confesses of herself and her collaborator, "This book is written almost entirely from selfish motives. We are not writing it mainly to delight our readers, but to delight ourselves — to give ourselves the pleasure of expressing ourselves at length on a subject which is completely absorbing to us both."

This of course is a sly way of saying that the authors adore Jane Austen, the subject of their work. We accept it and settle in for a treat. Very personal statements in a preface are, however, dangerous; only a master may indulge. The end of Maurois's foreword to *Prometheus* is genuinely touching in this respect; when he wrote it he was eighty. "Age," he says, "does not allow me to embark upon any more large undertakings or very extensive researches. This biography is the last I shall write. I am happy that the subject is Balzac."

A preface can be useful for specific explanation, not only concerning the author's credentials or the book's substance, but to explain the form and format, tell why the writer chose the narrative style, why he has not held (for instance) to strict chronology, or why — as with Burnett's *Continental Congress,* he decided to omit footnotes. Making over a series of lectures into book form presents special problems, which more than one biographer has faced. Shall he rewrite the whole, leaving out the asides, the direct addressing of the audience? To do so would seem proper, yet it can suck the life from a text and leave it dry. In a preface to that classic entitled *Foundations of American Constitutionalism,* Andrew C. McClaughlin gives his own solution — bland, serious, academic, forthright: "I have adhered in this volume to the lecture form of address and have not changed to the essay form. For this reason, and probably also because of my experiences in nearly half a century of teaching, I have allowed myself to indulge in emphasis and repetition, the common and useful devices of the classroom. My hope is that these characteristics will not be unwelcome in the printed page."

Already the reader is in a forgiving mood. Never mind how the professor writes it, this book has something to say.

Most writers, delivering their manuscript to the publisher, feel timidity, despair, or a defiance which is compounded of the two. They are glad to be rid of this incubus yet they hate to loose their brainchild to a cold censorious world. When thirty years ago I attempted the biography of my first lawyer I began at once a file of prefatory statements by authors who also had ventured outside their proper "fields." (My field at the time was far from the law.) Whether these authors wrote two centuries ago or yesterday was not my concern, and the more celebrated they were as writers, the better. Nor did it matter that I could never equal or even imitate them. The point was, they too had been brash in their attempt and they knew it. When Sir Thomas Browne, by profession a physician, set out to write *The Garden of Cyrus,* he was impelled to confess — inimitably — that he never was master of any considerable garden, nor would he have attempted this subject, had he not observed "that Purblind men have discoursed well of sight, and some without issue, excellently of Generation."

Again, it was a delight to find Jean Jacques Rousseau — a far less modest character — saying much the same in the preface to his *Social Contract:* "I enter upon my task without proving the importance of the subject. I shall be asked if I am a prince or a legislator, to write on politics. I answer that I am neither, and that is why I do so. If I were a prince or a legislator, I should not waste time in saying what wants doing; I should do it, or hold my peace." But it was a nineteenth-century legal historian who spoke to my condition most directly. William Stubbs, a bishop of the Church of England, wrote a whole shelf-ful of books on the constitutional history of his country. In one of them he says it will perhaps be asked why a bishop of the Church elects to write about the law. And then he remarks that "if a man wishes to learn something of a subject, his best policy is to write a book upon it."

Every author — perhaps every serious worker in any field — sooner or later comes across some word from a master of his craft, which lifts him off the ground and gives wings to his journey. In another Introduction, this time to his three-volume *Constitutional History of England,* Stubbs has an apologia for legal history itself, containing so much eloquence and good sense that it stays forever in the memory: "The History of Institutions cannot be mastered, — can scarcely be approached, — without an effort. It affords little of the romantic incident or of the picturesque grouping which constitute the charm of History in general, and holds out small temptation to the mind that requires to be tempted to the study of truth."

The mind that requires to be tempted. . . . Surely this is a legitimate goal for biographers — to hold out such temptation, persuade men to study the truth, and remember it. The roots of the present lie deep in the past, Stubbs said, "and nothing in the past is dead to the man who would learn how the present comes to be what it is." Ah, but it is dead, dead as any beetle on its back, until somebody re-creates it, calls it to life. Constitutional history lights no bivouac fires and contains, indeed, no clash and glare of arms and armies. Yet one asked oneself, could not the history of a constitution be told in terms of the men who helped to make it? After all, not robots but men — fallible, hopeful, quarrelsome, greedy, generous — sat at their tables in the Pennsylvania State House and wrote the United States Constitution in the year 1787. Which of these were timeservers and which, statesmen; was there truly a hero among them? What of Washington who presided in silence, what of James Madison who talked and talked and studied governments past and present? Fifty-five delegates had left their plantations and their businesses to sit in the city heat and hammer out a plan of government. Were they acting for their individual personal benefit and if so, is not that as good a reason, impulse, urge, as any other, providing the perpetrators are decent men?

When there is a plot to unravel or characters to establish and understand, readers can be induced to plough through some very dusty pages. With *Miracle at Philadelphia,* the preface, I told myself, must indeed draw in, persuade, seduce. It must let readers know there is strife ahead, and the exhibition of mortal passions — matters which can make an old story as new as Monday morning.

All my prefaces, as I wrote them, seemed to me intrinsic parts of the books in question. From a practical standpoint therefore it might be helpful to list some of the prefatorial problems I faced. Sir Francis Bacon was a subject whose name is known to every educated person, yet who is scarcely read today beyond his slim book of *Essays.* A prologue entitled "Lord Bacon's Reputation" reminded readers that the great philosopher was a man of two distinct careers: a lawyer who became lord chancellor, and a thinker who is known today as one of the fathers of modern scientific method. With John Adams a foreword told why my story ended in 1776, fifty years before the hero's death, yet there was to be no sequel. As for Justice Holmes, my narrative opened in 1800, with Holmes's grandfather writing his *Annals of America,* whereas the subject himself was not born until 1841, eight chapters later. When I sent the first seven chapters to my agent in New York, Harold Ober, saying I hoped he would like them, he wrote back asking how he could like or dislike seven chapters about a man who wasn't so much as born.

I could not have readers asking such a question; a preliminary statement must explain that here was a man whose presence carried tradition and whose story began in the New England of his forefathers.

In truth, most introductions are, at base, inducements, invitations — apologies if you will — no matter what their tone. "To make anything one writes public . . . is giving everybody leave under one's own hand to call one a fool." Thus Wilmarth Lewis in *Collector's Progress,* quoting Horace Walpole to express what authors feel when at the end of a book they sit down to compose a preface. Old Dr. Oliver Wendell Holmes was pleasingly explicit about this. His *Professor at the Breakfast Table* went through three editions, each with its foreword. In the final issue of 1891, the Doctor, looking back, notes that the first preface to a book is apt to be "explanatory, perhaps apologetic." He says there is "an anxious look about it. The author thinks he will be misapprehended about this or that matter . . . attacked as destructive by the conservatives and reproached for his timidity by the noisier radicals. After a time," the Doctor goes on, "the writer has cooled down from his excitement and is pleased to find that his book is still read, and that he must write a new Preface. He comes smiling to his task. How many things have explained themselves in the ten or twenty or thirty years since he came before his untried public in those almost plaintive paragraphs in which he introduced himself to his readers, — for the Preface writer, no matter how fierce a combatant he may prove, comes on the stage with his shield on his right arm and his sword in his left hand."

Currently there is among young writers a bitter turning away from what is called "the pressure to please," especially in the theater. If to please means to do less than one's best or to "write down" to one's readers, then the more savagely the writer turns away, the better. Yet there is a catch to this. Because even as the rebel artist screams his hatred of the public or of money-making — hit plays, best-selling books — his very screams communicate and he knows it. There can be hypocrisy in rebellion as in conformity, and the artist who aims to shock must reach his public before he can shock it.

To despise the world, despise life and mankind in general is very, very different from despising one's audience. The hating artist, like the loving artist, must communicate, make himself heard, read, looked at, felt.

142

Consciousness of this informs every preface, from Shakespeare's fool in motley bowing before the curtain to a biography of the latest visitor to Russia or outer space. In 1650, John Hacket wrote a life of Lord Chancellor Williams. Author and subject are today forgotten. Yet I think the words of Hacket's preface have not been bettered as expressing that mixture of anxiety, hope and stout acknowledgment of purpose which drives every biographer to his book:

"How shall I defend that I am constant to mine own judgment in this design, that I thrust my labours into the world? What warrant can I plead, that I build a new cottage upon the waste? . . . measuring my strength by my own meet-wand, I task myself to set up a pillar but for one man's memory."

15.

 *few words about talent*

This book has been concerned with technique, with ways and means of expression. Yet though the writing of biography is, on the face of it, a matter of conscious contrivance and planning — as is any work of art — I would not leave the impression of authors sitting for years and cannily fitting one paragraph into another paragraph, putting little boxes into bigger boxes — in short, that a good book is written simply by virtue of knowing all the tricks.

Inspiration is a flimsy subject for discussion. When, after a lecture, students inquire about inspiration (and they nearly always do) I am apt to dismiss the matter by suggesting that if a person has inspiration he will know it and if he has not he won't miss it. Justice Holmes, lecturing at the Harvard Law School, used to tell his students they could do anything they wanted in life, if only they wanted to hard enough. "But what I did not tell them," he added later, "was that they had to be born wanting to." It is an astringent thought, with a corollary in Holmes's remark that "if a man is adequate in native force he will be happy no matter what fate holds in store."

The persons who worry about talent are of course those who do not possess it. The talented ones worry over how to get the work done or how old they will be before the world appreciates them. What the young desire is a chance to use their strength; competition does not depress them but stimulates. "It is for this reason," said Woodrow Wilson, "that men are in love with power and greatness; it affords them so pleasurable an expansion of faculty, so large a run for their minds, an exercise of spirit so varied and reaching." Theodore Roosevelt as an old man was asked how he managed to combine in one life the writing of books, the career of a Rough Rider, big game hunter, editor of *The Outlook* magazine, politician and President of the United States. "I put myself in the way of things happening," he said; "and they happened."

Genius cannot be explained, though the world will never cease to try. Freud, Rank, Reik: a score of psychiatrists have searched the question. They have written books about it and drawn graphs to measure, for instance, musical talent, dividing it into component parts numbering five. They have collected data concerning the family background of famous men and women; one such book traces five hundred of these, all set out in view.

How much of artistic production is due to circumstance, how much to the original gene? Your person of talent and force grows with his success, whereas lesser talent lets itself be diverted by small triumphs. Dr. Frederick Allen, the psychiatrist, told me he had noted in his practice that for most people success is harder to bear than failure. It was Woodrow Wilson, again, who remarked that many a man has been ruined by his secondary successes. Brahms wrote his publisher, concerning Max Bruch the violinist, "Bruch is shortsighted. He sees only to the next laurel wreath." Brahms composed enough string quartets, he himself said, to paper a room. Of these he submitted only three for publication. One afternoon in a Vienna café, a young composer whose opera was to be performed, expressed fear of the critics. "Ach!" Brahms said. "It's customary to drown the first litter."

Brahms had a right to so harsh a view, having destroyed his own offspring when he considered them unworthy. The alternate toughness and softness of great artists, their persistence and their despair — to the biographer these are matters of endless fascination. What propelled these men? What kept them on the track, that hazardous rough track which they rode in sickness and in health, in poverty or good fortune or utmost wretchedness? Said Schubert, "My music is the child of my genius and my misery; that which I have written in my greatest distress is what the world appears to like the best."

One cannot read such a statement without marvel and curiosity. Forty years ago I began collecting bits of evidence about genius. If the phenomenon cannot be explained, I thought, at least it can be illustrated in terms of what genius has said about itself. Yet I made my collection not so much for use in future biographical chapters as because I could not let these statements pass and be forgotten. I wanted them near me, available, popping up when my heart failed — tacked above the desk, scribbled somewhere within sight or reach. And indeed these words and slogans, these noble cries of despair or triumph have served me well, and I am grateful. To me it has never seemed immodest to compare oneself to the great. Actually it is not a comparison but rather a measuring of oneself, as John Adams used to do when he set up great models and then scolded himself for falling short. How else can one learn, and how do children learn to speak?

The biographer, in the course of years spent with gifted subjects, is in a position to observe with some intimacy the conditions under which men produce their best works and function at their highest and happiest. In this final chapter, then, I have set out certain confessions of the great and the near great, from Serov and Moscheles, musicians, to several Presidents of the United States — and Francis Bacon. There was no feasible way to classify the quotations; I have simply strung them along as the text developed. Readers will have their own favorite quotations and no doubt will wonder why Keats, for instance, is not included, or "that thing Churchill said about the beaches." I can only answer that from a large and heterogeneous collection the words quoted are those which have come my way and have meant much to me.

One trait all genius has in common. Your person of unusual ability is aware of his powers. Said Joseph Haydn to a friend, "I know that God has bestowed a talent upon me, and I thank Him for it." Someone protested the gaiety of Haydn's church music. "I cannot help it," Haydn replied. "I give forth what is in me. When I think of the Divine Being, my heart is so full of joy that the notes fly off as from a spindle. And as I have a cheerful heart, He will pardon me if I serve Him cheerfully."

Self-knowledge comes early to the great. From then on it is a question of persuading the world to share this recognition. Fame however does not make creation easier; it has been said that what the general earns is not a silk tent but command. In the arts, the more one knows and the more one's technique increases, the higher one's standards rise. Near the top the view is wider but the rarified air makes climbing harder. Joyce Cary has said, in reference to painting:

> the more experienced [the painter] is, the more accomplished and subtle, the more care he will take. Manet would scrape off his paint day after day until, after fifty trials, he could satisfy himself that no further improvement was possible. That is,

he was not merely expressing an intuition, he was
continually discovering new possibilities in his
own work, now become objective to him, and
realizing them. The whole process was one of ex-
ploration as well as expression.

Said Rudyard Kipling:

Thus, then, I made my own experiments in the
weights, colours, perfumes and attributes of words
in relation to other words, either as read aloud so
that they may hold the ear, or, scattered over the
page, draw the eye. There is no line of my verse or
prose which has not been mouthed till the tongue
has made all smooth, and memory, after many
recitals, has mechanically skipped the grosser
superfluities.

Genius frequently explains itself, and with utmost
seriousness, in terms of technique. Tchaikovsky called
inspiration a guest that does not visit lazy people. He
once wrote to a friend:

Since I began to compose, I have made it my object
to be, in my craft, what the most illustrious masters
were in theirs; that is to say, I want to be, like
them, an artisan, just as the shoemaker is. . . .
They compose their immortal works exactly as a
shoemaker makes shoes; that is to say, day in and
day out, and for the most part to order.
For me, as a creative musician, composition is a
daily function that I feel compelled to discharge. I

suppose that I am made for that and cannot do otherwise. Just as any organ atrophies unless kept in a state of constant activity, so the faculty of composition becomes enfeebled and dulled unless kept up by effort and practice. The uninitiated imagine one must wait inspiration in order to create. That is a mistake. I am far from saying there is no such thing as inspiration; quite the opposite. It is found as a driving force in every kind of human activity, and is in no wise peculiar to artists. But that force is only brought into action by an effort, and that effort is work. Just as appetite comes by eating, so work brings inspiration, if inspiration is not discernible in the beginning. But it is not simply inspiration that counts; it is the result of inspiration — that is, the composition.

The principal reason I chose Tchaikovsky as a biographical subject was this extraordinary objectivity toward his work — even more remarkable considering the intensely personal, emotional nature of his music. Tchaikovsky's letters to Nadejda von Meck express not only the torments of an abnormally sensitive nature in conflict with circumstance. More importantly, they delineate with wonderful clarity the technical problems of composition. Yet always Tchaikovsky showed the artist's discipline; spiritual distress was not permitted to dam the musical creative flow. Tchaikovsky's biography happened to be my first; I confess that the quotations copied from my subject's letters were kept within reach not only for use in future chapters but to bolster my

spirit in a difficult task. I confess also that I kept in sight
J. S. Bach's magnificent reply, when asked the secret of
his mastership. "I worked hard," he said.

The spirits of the great are pervasive. After writing
the biography of Sinclair Lewis, Mark Schorer said,

> I am not a better man, certainly, for having
> written his life; but I think that I am a wiser one.
> And I can only hope that my gratitude to him for
> that will lighten a little the onus of the life with
> which I have burdened him.

Biographers are well aware of the spiritual debt they
owe to their heroes. I believe they all share the feeling
of responsibility expressed by Schorer. Would the subject approve this biography, would he think it just and
fair? If we should meet him in some future world,
would he extend the hand of friendship? The biographer in truth lives surrounded by ghosts; the spirits of
the dead and the truly great are near him as he writes.

One of the most remarkable revelations received
from these biographical heroes is their psychological and
spiritual dependence on *work*, not merely in the way of
earning money but as a means of preserving health and
sanity. Great artists are set apart by their talent. They
know they are not as other men, and this apparently is
no comfortable feeling. Work and work only — painting, writing, composing music — gives them a blessed
conviction of function in a world which they feel is
alien. Work tells them they can be themselves — unique,
defiant — yet share with and contribute to the life

around them. Thomas Carlyle said it is the worker who possesses the secret of life. Freud declared:

> Laying stress upon importance of work has a greater effect than any other technique of living in the direction of binding the individual more closely to reality; in his work he is at least securely attached to a part of reality, the human community. Work is no less valuable . . . because it is indispensable for subsistence and justifies its existence in society.

Gamaliel Bradford's journal presents like testimony, but given spontaneously, almost a cry of joy with an apology at the end as a sop to the devil. "I live and live only," Bradford says, "in the world of my work, and where else or how else could I live that would be more delightful? The drawback — since there always is one — is my own sense of my work's woeful deficiencies."

Through work, then, the artist retains his spiritual freedom and serenity. Benedetto Croce has defined peace as "harmonious, coherent, self-confident labor and exertion." And Spinoza said that freedom "is the understanding of the necessity of one's own nature."

The relationship between himself and his work is to the great artist so close that for his part the two are all but indistinguishable. What he has written or painted is one with his blood and bone. Who can forget Beethoven's magnificent irony, his heroic jest when, just before his final illness, the doctors were drawing water from his dropsical stomach. "Better from my belly than

my pen!" said Beethoven. Flaubert, writing the death
scene of Madame Bovary, said he felt the bitter poison
in his own mouth. Beer-Hofmann, the Austrian poet,
has testified that after writing the scene of Jacob wrestling with the angels (in *Jacob's Dream*), he felt himself
limping when he rose from his desk.

Artists are apt to be well or ill according to how their
work fares, so that physical symptoms often enough
reveal the pangs or joys of creation. Sir George
Henschel, conductor of the Boston Symphony Orchestra
and founder of the London Symphony Concerts, for a
while took piano lessons from Moscheles — an artist
who, though no genius, possessed extraordinary virtu-
osity and won much applause in his day. Said Moscheles
to his pupil,

> When I wrote my piano concerto with three
> kettle drums, I came to a tutti which I wanted
> rather fully and noisily orchestrated. Well — will
> you believe, I heard that tutti and the noise of the
> different instruments so distinctly whilst I was
> writing it, that — that I got a headache!

The extreme sensitivity of artists has been often
noted, yet seldom with more good sense and clarity than
in Walter Bagehot's words:

> Men of genius are in general distinguished by
> their extreme susceptibility to external experience.
> Finer and softer than other men, every exertion of
> their will, every incident of their lives, influences
> them more deeply than it would others. Their

essence is at once finer and more impressible; it receives a distincter mark, and receives it more easily than the souls of the herd. From a peculiar sensibility, the man of genius bears the stamp of life more clearly than his fellows; even casual associations make a deep impression on him.

The roster is long of celebrated persons who in spite of lingering and painful illness did their work and did it well. The poet Heine, Prescott, Parkman . . . Gamaliel Bradford for twenty years suffered attacks of vertigo which literally threw him from his chair to the floor; there were times when he lay in a darkened room for thirteen consecutive hours. Yet his zest for work remained:

> I look forward with passionate eagerness to finishing my task. The theme is so boiling in my head that I should like to tear it all out at once and get it all on the paper in a day to two days, instead of looking forward to months of it. Just compare such infantile restlessness with the colossal persistence of Darwin, the waiting twenty years before committing anything to paper at all, so as to make sure that the whole investigation was complete and as it should be. That is the way really great work is to be done.
>
> The absurd varieties of nervous torment which I have suffered in the course of my life would indeed make a curious volume, if they could be written down. And the question I ask myself again and

again is whether normal people, out of insane asylums, generally suffer such or whether they are peculiar to me. Do the quiet, comfortable-looking men and women, whom I see about me, all, or mostly, carry such a hell of fret and annoyance within them as I do?

The answer is, No, Mr. Bradford, they do not. And while certain of them would doubtlessly look on you as crazy, there are others who would call it the quality of heroism.

Leon Edel wrote of Proust:

How simple then to mock this figure — to call him "sick, sick, sick," and to murmur, "neurotic art" and therefore sick art. But would this not be — has it not been — an enormous failure in perception? Proust the man was sick, Proust the artist was strong, healthy, assertive; he was more triumphant over veritably crushing forces and demonstrated a greater will for survival and a capacity for *life* than many of the living. . . . Remember that even as Proust lay dying he was revising passages in his work dealing with the death of Bergotte. These are the victories of the human spirit over the forces of defeat.

In gifted persons the sense of life that Edel speaks of is very strong. Great artists seem in love with life; every day they endure the alternate ecstasy and anguish of a love affair. Wrote Berlioz:

Reasonable people do not know to what degree the feeling of existence may attain; the heart dilates, the imagination takes an immense flight, one lives with fury.

Serov, the composer, confided to his sister in a letter:

For me the most important thing of all is — *life!* Let life only be stamped in sufficiently sharp outline and I rejoice, even when I feel it painfully and in the unhappiness of those dear to me. If that is peculiar, it is the peculiarity of an artistic nature, which always seeks joy in spectacle, even if the spectacle be that of its own sufferings.

Albert Camus declared:

There is a will to live without rejecting anything of life, which is the virtue I honor most in this world.

The artist seems to know instinctively that in proportion to his sense of life, his sympathy with life, his work will be great. Martha Graham is here referring to dancers, but what she says applies equally to the writer, the painter or musician:

There is a vitality, a life-force, an energy, a quickening which is translated through you into action, and because there is only one of you in all time, this expression is unique. And if you block it, it will never exist through any other medium and be lost. The world will not have it.

Something Sir Thomas Browne said has remained with me since the day I read it long ago. This quiet seventeenth-century physician did not sound the romantic overtones of a Berlioz or a Graham, but he expresses much the same in his own unexampled way as he measures the beat of his existence. "Since," he says,

> thou hast an Alarum in thy breast which tells thee thou hast a living Spirit in thee above two thousand times an hour. . . .

Equated with and related to this consciousness of the life force is the trait of originality, so striking in persons of genius and so disturbing to the artist's immediate environment and those who have to do with him. "Originality," said John Stuart Mill, "is the one thing which unoriginal minds cannot feel the use of."

Thomas Carlyle wrote of his hero, Oliver Cromwell,

> This man is of the sort we now call original men, men of genius or such like; the first peculiarity of which is that they in some measure converse with the universe at first-hand . . . these have ever, deny it as we will, a kind of divine worth for us.

This essential quality of genius has been called by various names. To William Blake it was *energy:*

Energy is the only life and is from the body; and reason is the outward circumference of energy. Energy is eternal delight.

If the energy and originality of genius startles ordinary people, so does the phenomenon of their abundance. Lesser talents produce sparely, though their production may be exquisite. But your true genius produces in shoals, in barrelsful, shelvesful, with the level of quality rising and falling, as witness Dickens, Thackeray, Tolstoi, Beethoven. To live in the house with great talent can be trying; certainly there is nothing restful about it. I knew such a man, who would come home after a day's work and hurl himself into a deep chair. "I'm EXHAUSTED!" he would shout, his voice ringing through the house and down the stairwell.

It has been said that all genius shows something of the monstrous, something of what Nietzsche called the "over-man." Maurois has spoken of the "healthy egotism of the creator which resembles so much that of the expectant mother." But I think Nietzsche came nearer the mark when he referred to the artist's egotism that shines like brass and will not be denied. The world resents this trait, moreover it creates an enigma: the master's output seems at war with his personality, though to himself there is no discrepancy. Rameau's music, for instance, is filled with the tenderest melody, the clearest and most melting harmonies. Yet those who knew the master said he had no heart; Diderot declared that Rameau's wife and daughter might die but he would not care provided the passing bell tolled in tune.

A few words about talent

Concerning the conditions under which artists do their best work, William James in his *Varieties of Religious Experience* has pointed out that different personalities seem to require differing degrees of hardship or ease in their personal life:

> Some men and women, indeed, there are who can live on smiles and the word "yes" forever. For others . . . this is too tepid and relaxed a moral climate. Some austerity and wintry negativity, some roughness, danger, stringency and effort, some no! no! must be mixed in, to produce the sense of an existence with character and texture and power. The range of individual difference in this respect is enormous; but whatever the mixture of yesses and noes may be, the person is infallibly aware when he has struck it in the right proportion *for him.* "This," he feels, "is my proper vocation, this is the *optimum,* the law, the life for me to live. Here I find the degree of equilibrium, safety, calm, and leisure which I need, or here I find the challenge, passion, fight and hardship without which my soul's energy expires.

Theodore Roethke, the poet, once said after much thought that what he needed in order to write was a sense of well-being when he got up in the morning. I think I know what he meant — a sense of his powers serving him, pulling together in all their native force. Robert Frost told me he could not write poetry if he heard that somebody had said something mean about him. Genius makes much noise and plaint about solitude and its necessity for creation. Let me alone, I must be alone! is the cry. Yet when these harried ones do succeed in isolating themselves, they panic. Rockwell Kent escaped to the northern tundra, and almost at once sent frantic messages to his friends to come and visit him. Artists show themselves uneasy when away from the familiar room, the desk, the studio where it has been their habit to create. Homesickness affects the greatly talented like a frenzy, a mania, as witness Tchaikovsky's letters from Italy or Paris.

Hector Berlioz was a man who managed his outward life successfully enough. Yet, writing of what he calls "loneliness and absence," his words are like a madman's:

> I do not know how to convey any adequate conception of this unutterable anguish. . . . There is a vacuum all round my throbbing breast, and I feel as if under the influence of some irresistible power my heart were evaporating and bending toward dissolution. My skin begins to pain and burn; I get hot all over; I feel an irresistible desire to call my friends and even strangers to help me, to protect me, to console me and preserve me from destruction, and to restrain the life which is being drawn out of me to the four quarters of the globe.

Wagner, exiled to Switzerland by his government, wrote to Liszt:

> All I want is sufficient *charm of life* to get into the indispensable cheerful mood from which

motifs spring forth gladly and spontaneously. . . . I have many things to tell you, but my head is burning. There is something wrong with me; and sometimes, with lightning-like rapidity, the thought flashes through me that it would be better, after all, if I died. But that has nothing to do with my writing music.

Matthew Arnold's receipt for artistic creation is expressed with a bland sophistication that is a little surprising in a poet:

The three things that improve genius; proper exertion, frequent exertion and successful exertion. . . . The three things that support genius: prosperity, social acquaintance and applause.

Henry James said he thought a position in society a legitimate object of ambition — a subtle Jamesian way of confessing, like Lamb and Trollope, that he liked to be liked. Charles Dickens was always defending himself, writing letters to the press about how he was misunderstood. Yet neither criticism nor misunderstanding stopped the flow. "Dickens," said G. K. Chesterton, "was the character whom anybody can hurt and nobody can kill." After the failure of his First Symphony, Rachmaninoff remained idle for a year, lying about on sofas without writing a note of music. He was twenty-two at the time. When Beethoven heard that a certain conductor refused to perform one of his works, he went to bed and stayed there until the symphony was played. Chopin all his life suffered from lack of confidence in his powers, that madness which in French is called the *folie de doute*. Before the jealous gods these gifted ones pour the libation of self-doubt. Among all the nine-teenth-century Romanticists of my collection, Wagner's cries are the most agonizing.

To Liszt, from exile in Switzerland:

> I cannot tell you too often how miserably weak I feel as a musician. I know, in the depths of my heart, that I am a blunderer. You ought to watch me when I am at it; now thinking, "it must do after all," then going to the piano to puzzle out some wretched rubbish, and giving it up, again in a sense of idiocy. Oh, how I feel then; how thoroughly persuaded of my musical wretchedness!

And again:

> Everything seems so waste, so lost! Dearest friend, art, with me, after all, is a pure stopgap, nothing else. It is therefore with genuine despair that I always resume art. The only thing I want is *money;* that, at least, one ought to be able to get. *Love,* I abandon, and *art!*

One sees the energy in such despair. And one notes that in spite of everything the work at hand is finished — perhaps in a Wagnerian frenzy, perhaps, as with Palestrina and Bach, in serenity, with the final inscription, *Soli Dei Gloria.* Carlyle, working on the *History of the French Revolution,* wrote in his Journal:

Chelsea. February 7, 1835.

The great difficulty is to keep one's self in right balance, not despondent, not exasperated, defiant, free and clear. . . .

Nevertheless it is now some three-and-twenty months since I have earned one penny by the craft of literature. . . . I have been ready to work, know no fault I have committed; and yet so it stands. To *ask* able editors to employ you will not improve but worsen matters. You are like a spinster waiting to be married.

February 8

Allein und abgetrennt von aller Freude! I repeated this morning. Yet thou canst write. Write then and complain of nothing — defy all things. The book announced yesterday. Would that I were further on with it!

And to his brother, John Carlyle:

In a word, my prospects here are not sensibly brightening. . . . In bright days I say it is *impossible* but I must by and by strike into something. In dark days I say, "and suppose nothing?" My sentiment is a kind of sacred defiance of the whole matter.

A sense of imminent fate hangs over artists. Something will happen to stop their work — accident, illness, death, or the blockage of their powers which for them is tantamount to extinction. "I must hurry, hurry," wrote Tchaikovsky. "I am afraid I shall die with all my music in me." Faulkner, walking the pavements of New York, looked over his shoulder. "I got a Doom follerin' me," he said. To great men, time is an enemy, pressing and pushing. Holmes quoted the Latin poet: "Death plucks my ear and says, 'Live! I am coming!' " Though Holmes was to live till ninety-three, at fifty-eight he felt the end approaching and said he heard "the roar of the cataract." Joseph Conrad too was convinced he would die early, bemoaned this sad oncoming fate and lived to a ripe age.

The urge and drive of their genius causes such men to hoard their time closely. "I am sorry I cannot accept your invitation," Holmes wrote. "But in order to get my work done I live on a routine as strict as a baby's." Tchaikovsky had a country villa at Klin, near Moscow. In 1937 I visited the house and saw a sign that used to hang outside the gate,

P. I. Tchaikovsky. Receives Mondays and Thursdays, 3 to 5. Otherwise, not at home. Please do not ring.

True genius knows its worth, and there is in the occasional frank confession of this knowledge a simplicity that is wonderfully refreshing.

Berlioz, at twenty-two:

I am not an amateur but an artist, and as such I can speak of my art with the assurance given by long studies, familiarity with the great masters, and profound reflection.

Beethoven, in a letter to Peters, the Leipsic publishers:

I adhere to the sum of 50 ducats, which is in fact nowadays the usual price for a string quartet. I feel positively ashamed when I have to ask a price for a really great work. Still, such is my position that it obliges me to secure every possible advantage. It is very different, however, with the work itself, when I never, thank God, think of profit, but solely of how I write it.

And again, from Beethoven:

I do not fear for my works. No evil can befall them; and whoever shall understand them, he shall be freed from the misery that burdens mankind.

This extraordinary statement can be tested, proven, only by listening to the music. Joyce Cary has said, in his book, *Art and Reality:*

A friend of mine tells me that a Beethoven symphony can solve for him a problem of conduct. I've no doubt that it does so simply by giving him a sense of the tragedy and the greatness of human destiny, which makes his personal anxieties seem small, which throws them into new proportion.

With what marvelous difference men of genius look upon themselves! Schopenhauer, for instance was a tremendous eater. A stranger, dining with him, showed astonishment at the performance. "Sir," said Schopenhauer, "I eat a great deal because I am a great man." Rudyard Kipling spoke affectionately of his Daemon:

> I learned to lean upon him and recognize the sign of his approach. If ever I held back, Ananias fashion, anything of myself (even if I had to throw it out afterwards) I paid for it by missing what I *then* knew the tale lacked. . . . My Daemon was with me in the *Jungle Books, Kim,* and both Puck books, and good care I took to walk delicately, lest he should withdraw. I know that he did not, because when those books were finished they said so themselves with, almost, the water-hammer click of a tap turned off. . . . When your Daemon is in charge, do not try to think consciously. Drift, wait, and obey.

It is a long way from Kipling to John Adams, who, with his Puritan background, could never confess his genius, even to himself. But at the age of twenty his diary reveals a fierceness of ambition and a consequent self-discipline not granted to lesser souls:

> I am resolved to rise with the sun. May I blush whenever I suffer one hour to pass unimproved. I will rouse up my mind and fix my attention; I will stand collected within myself and think upon what I read and what I see.

To stand collected within oneself and think on what one reads and sees. . . . It is a bold prescription; few men of fifty would dare as much, let alone a youth of twenty. The significant thing is that Adams followed it, his whole life bears it out. A great man in his youth makes large declarations or dreams wide dreams; we know that we have only to wait to see the promises made good. Francis Bacon had no scruples about declaring himself to the universe or to anyone who would listen. In his early thirties, still a worldly failure but supremely confident of his intellectual powers, Bacon wrote his celebrated uncle, Lord Treasurer Burghley, a letter that has become part of history:

> My Lord . . . I wax now somewhat ancient; one and thirty years is a great deal of sand in the hour-glass. I confess that I have vast contemplative ends . . . for I have taken all knowledge to be my province.

And that, actually, is what Sir Francis did.

Between artistic challenge and physical challenge there is more affinity than one is at first willing to believe. When I had been working for five years on Coke's biography I happened to read in a magazine Roger Bannister's account of how he ran the first four-minute mile. Every word applied to my condition and seemed to have been written for me. No matter if the comparison is ridiculous between a woman trying to finish a sedentary task and a young athlete gasping out his lungs in a race — I think any writer who has planned a long book, spaced it, wrestled with it month on month and come at last toward the end, would feel a like response.

Bannister's account tells of the years of preparation and training, then of the race itself, which was run at Oxford in 1954. When he was three hundred yards from the finish —

> I had a moment of mixed joy and anguish [Bannister writes] when my mind took over. It raced well ahead of my body and drew it compellingly forward. I felt that the moment of a lifetime had come. I drove on, impelled by a combination of fear and pride. Those last few moments seemed never ending. The faint line of the finishing tape stood ahead as a haven of peace after the struggle. The arms of the world were waiting to receive me, if only I reached it without slackening my speed. If I faltered, there would be no arms to hold me and the world would be a cold, forbidding place because I had been so close. I leapt at the tape like a man taking his last spring to save himself from the chasm that threatens to engulf him.

With young Bannister then we take our leave of the talented, the greatly gifted, who embrace all risks implicit to their ambition. Driven to compete or impelled to communicate, they do not spare themselves in acquiring the techniques of their art. What they have done and what they have said can be for the rest of us a part of the learning process.

Index

Pierce, William, 78
Polk, James K., 60
Pope, Alexander, 45
Prescott, Hilda F. M., xi, 42, 76, 102, 121–122
Prescott, William H., 154
Proust, Marcel, 44, 155

Rachmaninoff, Sergei, 161
Ralegh, Sir Walter, 15, 37–38, 42, 50–51, 67, 74–75, 79, 86, 106, 109–111, 112–114, 127
Rameau, Jean Philippe, 158
Rank, Otto, 145
Read, Conyers, 64, 129, 135
Reik, Theodor, 45, 145
Rembrandt, Harmensz van Rijn, 35
Renan, Ernest, 40
Revere, Paul, 98–99
Rinehart, Mary Roberts, xii–xiii
Roethke, Theodore, 159
Roosevelt, Theodore, 145
Rousseau, Jean Jacques, 138–139
Rubinsteins, Anton and Nicholas, 97
Rush, Dr. Benjamin, 25

Sand, George, 10, 103–104
Sandburg, Carl, 12
Sandwich, Fourth Earl of, 114–115
Sazanov, Sergei, 83
Schopenhauer, Arthur, 166
Schorer, Mark, 151
Schubert, Franz Peter, 147
Serov, Alexander, 147, 156
Shakespeare, William, 69, 143
Shelley, Percy Bysshe, 34, 44

Sherman, Roger, 79
Simmons, Ernest, 111
Sitwell, Edith, 22–23
Spanish Armada, 71, 93
Spinoza, Benedict de, 152
Staats Bibliotheke, 25
Stanley, Sir Henry Morton, 101
Stern, G. B., 14
Strachey, Lytton G., 13, 41, 45
Strateman, Catherine, 122–123
Stuart, Gilbert, 84
Stubbs, William, 139
Sukhomlinov, Vladimir A., 83

Tchaikovsky, Peter Ilyich, 16, 27–28, 43, 67, 97, 98, 149–150, 160, 164
Thackeray, William Makepeace, 158
Tolstoi, Leo, 82, 111, 158
Trevelyan, George Macauley, 51, 75
Trollope, Anthony, 41, 161
Troyat, Henri, 82
Tuchman, Barbara, 82–83
Twain, Mark, 64

Van Doren, Carl, 93
Verulam, Baron and Viscount St. Albans. *See* Sir Francis Bacon
Victoria of England, 45, 101, 128

Wagner, Wilhelm Richard, 160–161, 162
Walpole, Horace, 141
Walsingham, Sir Francis, 71
Walton, Izaak, 136
Washington, George, 46, 70–71, 79, 83–85, 88, 90, 120, 140

Index

Webster, Noah, 87
Webster-Parkman murder, 94
Wedgwood, C. V., xii, 65, 103
Weems, Parson, 84, 120

Wilson, Woodrow, 145–146
Wood, Anthony à, 135–136
Woodham-Smith, Cecil, 92
Wythe, George, 95